Writing Fiction offers the novice writer engaging and creative activities, making use of insightful, relevant readings from well-known authors to illustrate the techniques presented. This volume makes use of new versions of key chapters from the recent Routledge/ Open University textbook *Creative Writing: A Workbook with Readings* for writers who are specialising in fiction.

Using their experience and expertise as teachers as well as authors, Linda Anderson and Derek Neale guide aspiring writers through such key aspects of writing as:

- how to stimulate creativity
- keeping a writer's notebook
- character creation
- setting
- point of view
- structure
- showing and telling.

The volume is further updated to include never-before published interviews with successful fiction writers Andrew Cowan, Stevie Davies, Maggie Gee, Andrew Greig and Hanif Kureishi. Concise and practical, *Writing Fiction* offers an inspirational guide to the methods and techniques of authorship and is a must-read for aspiring writers.

Linda Anderson is an award-winning novelist and is editor of *Creative Writing, A Workbook with Readings* (2006, Routledge). She is Reader in Creative Writing at the Open University and a National Teaching Fellow.

Derek Neale is Lecturer in Creative Writing at The Open University. He is an award-winning fiction writer and is editor of *A Creative Writing Handbook* (2009) and co-author of *Life Writing* (2008, Routledge).

RELATED TITLES FROM ROUTLEDGE AND THE OPEN UNIVERSITY

Life Writing
Linda Anderson and Derek Neale

This practical guide covers key life writing skills including writing what you know, biography and autobiography, prefaces, form, memory, characters, and novelistic, poetic and dramatic techniques. *Life Writing* presents never-before published interviews with successful life writers such as Jenny Diski, Robert Fraser, Richard Holmes, Michael Holroyd, Jackie Kay, Hanif Kureishi and Blake Morrison.

ISBN13: 978–0–415–46153–5 (pbk)
December 2008

Writing Poetry
Bill Herbert

Concise and highly useful, *Writing Poetry* offers a clearly written, inspirational guide to methods and techniques of poetry, covering drafting, line, voice, imagery, rhyme, form and theme. This volume presents never-before published interviews with poets such as Vicki Feaver, Douglas Dunn, Gillian Allnutt, Jo Shapcott, Kathleen Jamie, Linda France and Sean O'Brien.

ISBN13: 978–0–415–46154–2 (pbk)
July 2009

Available at all good bookshops
For ordering and further information please visit:
www.routledgeliterature.com

Writing Fiction

Linda Anderson and Derek Neale

Routledge
Taylor & Francis Group

LONDON AND NEW YORK

First edition published 2009
by Routledge
2 Park Square, Milton Park, Abingdon, Oxon, OX14 4RN

Simultaneously published in the USA and Canada
by Routledge
711 Third Avenue, New York, NY 10017

Routledge is an imprint of the Taylor & Francis Group, an informa business

© 2009 Linda Anderson and Derek Neale

Typeset in Frutiger and Times by RefineCatch Limited, Bungay, Suffolk

British Library Cataloguing in Publication Data
A catalogue record for this book is available from the British Library

Library of Congress Cataloging-in-Publication Data
Anderson, Linda.
Writing fiction/Linda Anderson and Derek Neale.—1st ed.
p. cm.
Includes bibliographical references and index.
1. Creative writing (Higher education)—Problems, exercises, etc.   2. Fiction—
Authorship—Problems, exercises, etc.   3. English language—Rhetoric—Study and
teaching.   4. Authorship—Problems, exercises, etc.   I. Neale, Derek.   II. Title.
PE1404.A5274 2008
808.3076—dc22
2008028834

ISBN13: 978-0-415-46155-9
ISBN10: 0-415-46155-3

Contents

Acknowledgements

The publisher and authors would like to thank the following for permission to reprint material under copyright:

Extract from 'The Dream', Anon, taken from N.J. Dawood (trans.) (1973) *Tales from the Thousand and One Nights*, London: Penguin. Translation copyright © 1995 by N.J. Dawood. Reproduced by permission of Penguin Books Ltd.

Extract from Lindsay Clarke, 'Going the Last Inch: Some thoughts on showing and telling' by Julia Bell and Paul Magrs (eds) (2001) *The Creative Writing Coursebook*, London: Macmillan. Copyright © 2001 by Lindsay Clark. Reproduced by permission of PFD (www.pfd.co.uk) on behalf of Lindsay Clarke.

'I could see the smallest things' from Raymond Carver (1985) *The Short Stories of Raymond Carver*, London: Picador/Pan Books. Copyright © 1985 by Raymond Carver. Reprinted with permission of The Wylie Agency, Inc.

Extracts from 'Pigeons at Daybreak' by Anita Desai (1978) *Games at Twilight and Other Stories*, London: Penguin. Copyright © 1978 by Anita Desai. Reproduced by permission of the author c/o Rogers, Coleridge & White Ltd., 20 Powis Mews, London W11 1JN.

Extracts from 'Writing Short Stories' by Flannery O'Connor (1970 [1957]) *Mystery and Manners: Occasional Prose* (Sally and Robert Fitzgerald, eds), New York: Farrar, Straus & Giroux. Reproduced by permission of PFD (www.pfd.co.uk) on behalf of Flannery O'Connor.

Extract from 'The Dying Room' from Georgina Hammick (1986) *People For Lunch*, London: Methuen. Reprinted by kind permission of the author and The Sayle Literary Agency.

Extract from Raymond Carver (1986 [1982]) *Fires*, London: Picador. Copyright © 1982 by Raymond Carver. Reprinted with permission of The Wylie Agency, Inc.

Extract from George Gissing (1983) *New Grub Street* (John Goode, ed.), Oxford: Oxford University Press. Copyright © 1993 by John Goode, Chronology of George Gissing © 1992 by Stephen Gill, Updated Bibliography © 1999 by David Grylls. Reprinted by permission of Oxford University Press.

Extract from W. Somerset Maugham (2001) *A Writer's Notebook*, London: Vintage. Reprinted by permission of A.P. Watt Ltd on behalf of The Royal Literary Fund and by kind permission of the Trustees of the W.S. Maugham Estate.

Extract from Susan Minot (2000) 'The Writing Life'. Copyright © 2000 by Susan Minot. Originally appeared in 'Book World', *The Washington Post* (16 January 2000). Reprinted by permission of Georges Borchardt Inc. on behalf of the author.

Extract from Bernard MacLaverty (1983) *Cal*, London: Jonathan Cape. Copyright © 1983 by Bernard MacLaverty. Reprinted by permission of The Random House Group Ltd, and of the author c/o Rogers, Coleridge & White Ltd., 20 Powis Mews, London W11 1JN.

Extract from P.F. Kluge (1996) *The Biggest Elvis*, London: Vintage. Reproduced by kind permission of The Random House Group Ltd and the author.

Extract from Jed Mercurio (2003) *Bodies*, London: Jonathan Cape. Copyright © 2003 by Jed Mercurio. Reproduced by permission The Random House Group Ltd, and of the author c/o Rogers, Coleridge & White Ltd., 20 Powis Mews, London W11 1JN.

Extracts from 'Mary Adare' and 'Sita Kozka' from Louise Erdrich (1987) *The Beet Queen*, London: HarperCollins. Copyright © 1986 by Louise

Erdrich. Reprinted by permission of Henry Holt and Company, and of HarperCollins Publishers Ltd

Extract from J.M. Coetzee (1991) *Age of Iron*, London: Penguin. Reproduced by permission of David Higham Associates Limited.

Extract from Pat Barker (1998) *Another World*, Harmondsworth: Viking (Farrar, Straus & Giroux edition, 1999). Copyright © 1998 by Pat Barker. Reproduced by permission of Penguin Books Ltd, of Farrar, Straus and Giroux, and of Aitken Alexander Associates Ltd.

Extract from John McGahern (11983) *The Dark*, London: Faber & Faber. Copyright © 1983 by John McGahern. Reprinted by permission of A.M. Heath & Co. Ltd.

Extract from 'Girl', by Jamaica Kincaid, *At the Bottom of the River*. Copyright © 1983 by Jamaica Kincaid. Reprinted by permission of Farrar, Straus & Giroux, and of The Wylie Agency, Inc.

Extract from Rick Moody (1997) *Purple America: A Novel*, London: Flamingo. Copyright © 1997 by Rick Moody. Reprinted by permission of Little, Brown & Company, and of Melanie Jackson Agency.

Extract from Andrew Miller, *Oxygen* (2001) London: Sceptre. Copyright © 2001 by Andrew Miller. Reproduced by permission of Hodder and Stoughton Ltd, and of Houghton Mifflin Harcourt Publishing Company.

Extract from Tim Lott (2002) *Rumours of a Hurricane*, Harmondsworth: Viking (Penguin Books, 2003). Copyright © 2002 by Tim Lott. Reproduced by permission of Penguin Books Ltd, and by kind permission of the author and Aitken Alexander Associates.

Every effort has been made to trace and contact copyright holders. The publishers would be pleased to hear from any copyright holders not acknowledged here, so that this acknowledgement page may be amended at the earliest opportunity.

Introduction

Linda Anderson and Derek Neale

One of the most daunting essay titles about writing fiction is 'Do You Have What It Takes to Become a Novelist?' It was written by John Gardner, who was, in fact, a great enabler and teacher of aspiring writers. But his title echoes exactly the kind of self-questioning and doubt that can hinder writers. Do I have enough talent? Enough time? Adequate life experience or education? Anything new or important to say?

Here's what Virginia Woolf said: 'What one wants for writing is habit' (quoted in Sher, 1999, p.18). This is a soothing prescription and it also happens to be true. That is why we begin this book with two chapters designed to help you get writing routinely and effortlessly. You will learn how to find those subjects that really interest you and how to start developing your material in a writer's notebook.

After this preparation period, we launch into a comprehensive guide to narrative craft with chapters on character, setting, point of view, showing and telling, structure, and a culminating chapter that explores genre, appropriate length, story types and the importance of the reader.

Writing Fiction is the work of two published authors who are also experienced writing tutors. We have designed and produced popular writing courses for the Open University and have taught the subject at Lancaster University and the University of East Anglia, which are both famous as producers of published writers.

This book features new versions of all relevant chapters from our acclaimed Open University course book, *Creative Writing: A Workbook with Readings*, which is used in many university and college courses and has achieved worldwide sales. We have revised the chapters specialising in fiction to integrate short illustrative readings. We also include extracts from interviews we have carried out with leading novelists about their personal approaches and strategies. Maggie Gee, Andrew Greig, Stevie Davies, Hanif Kureishi, and Andrew Cowan share successful methods from their own practice.

The book's method is highly practical. It is designed to help you generate your own abundant stack of material in response to suggestions and exercises. The keeping of a writer's notebook is a key strategy and should be begun early on. Your notebook is where you can store your observations, responses and experiments – it acts as a spur to both imagination and commitment. Each chapter of the book contains several writing exercises. Their purpose is to give you immediate practice in whatever aspects of writing are being discussed. They are not tests – they are meant to be enjoyable, doable, sometimes provocative or challenging. If you dislike an exercise, try it anyway. Sometimes irritation or resistance can mobilise creativity in surprising ways. You may find that some exercises will deliver more than an addition to your repertoire of techniques. You may come up with the seed of a narrative, some fictional character who will lodge in your imagination, some scene that will start to suggest a whole story, or a personal memory that you can use in a new way. In these cases, the exercises are a scaffolding that falls away to reveal new work. The book contains a few exercises which are involved with producing longer projects but the majority of the exercises are designed to take between 10 and 45 minutes. If you enjoy a particular exercise, you may want to devote more time to it or return to it and try out variations. If you find yourself working on an exercise for several hours, rejoice – it's no longer an exercise but on its way to being a story or chapter.

This book is appropriate for use on courses or by writers' groups or by individual writers working alone. It is suitable for aspiring writers who have begun to try things out as well as for more experienced writers who want to deepen their skills or seek new directions for their work. It may be worked through sequentially or used as a resource book for both writers and writing tutors to dip in to as needed. If you are a writer working on your own, you may wonder how to gauge the effectiveness of your writings. The discussion sections after each activity give some guidance on how to review what you've done. Put your work away for a while, and then read it with fresh eyes.

The most important aim of *Writing Fiction* is to help you to discover and nurture your individual voice as a fiction writer. In each chapter you will find lots of advice about writing but you do not have to take it. There are no 'rules' or prescriptions. There is no 'right' way to carry out the exercises, only your own best and truest way.

When you have mastered narrative craft, you will find yourself moving deeper into your stories with greater ease and excitement. Familiarity with technique can free you to enter unexpected territory more quickly – those moments of strangeness and newness or sudden insight that make the act of writing so thrilling and rewarding. Charles Baxter describes this experience as 're-cognition' – knowing something afresh:

> It's like that moment when, often early in the morning, perhaps in a strange house, you pass before a mirror you hadn't known would be there. You see a glimpse of someone reflected in that mirror, and a moment passes before you recognize that that person is yourself. Literature exists in moments like that.
>
> (Baxter 1997: 49, 50)

This is an eloquent reminder that fictional truth emerges from the realm of the unconscious rather than from technique and intellect alone. Techniques are essential but they are only a means – the gateway, not the destination. We hope that working your way through this book will increase not just your technical range but also your imaginative reach.

References

Baxter, Charles (1997) *Burning Down the House: Essays on fiction*, Minnesota: Graywolf Press.

Sher, Gail (1999) *One Continuous Mistake: Four noble truths for writers*, London: Penguin Arkana.

1

Stimulating creativity and imagination: what really works?

Linda Anderson

Writers speak a lot about the 'blank page' – usually the daunting emptiness of it or, sometimes, the lure of it. How do writers get started afresh each day, facing the pristine pages or the empty screen?

Let's look first at two opening sentences. These are the habitual starting points used by two novelists at the beginning of their daily practice. One of the novelists is a fictional character and the other is a real living writer.

Can you guess which sentence was written by an imaginary character and which by an actual author?

> One fine morning in the month of May an elegant young horse-woman might have been seen riding a handsome sorrel mare along the flowery avenues of the Bois de Boulogne.

> The quick brown fox jumps over the lazy dog.

The first sentence is one version of the constantly reworked opening of a novel by Joseph Grand, a somewhat comic figure in Albert Camus's *The Plague* (1960 [1947]), which explores the impact of an outbreak of bubonic plague on the inhabitants of the imaginary town of Oran. Joseph Grand is an aspiring novelist who devotes all of his spare time and energies to writing. He is impelled by the dream of a publisher reading his work and being so thunderstruck that he stands up and says to his staff, 'Hats off, gentlemen!' (Camus 1960 [1947]: 98), which conjures the faintly surreal vision of publishers sitting in offices wearing their hats. But Grand can never progress beyond his first sentence. He worries at every detail of it, ponders the derivation and meaning of words, frets over the tastefulness, the rhythms, the factual accuracy. Is 'sorrel' really a colour? Are there really any flowers in the Bois de Boulogne? He makes minor alterations, never satisfied. And of course, the sentence doesn't work – we see the writer's fussy effort more than the scene itself.

The second sentence is the well-known line which uses all twenty-six letters of the alphabet. In volume two of her autobiography, New Zealand writer Janet Frame (1984) describes how she started her daily writing sessions by typing this sentence repeatedly when she was creating her first novel. After a long period of hospitalisation during which she endured over two hundred electro-convulsive shock treatments, 'each the equivalent, in degree of fear, to an execution' (Frame 1984: 112), she was living in the home of Frank Sargeson, an established author who took her under his wing. Each morning she went into a garden hut to write, while her mentor pottered about outside, tending his plants. Desperate to appear gratefully industrious she would type that line, alternating it with 'Now is the time for all good men to come to the aid of the party' (Frame 1984: 144). There was no 'theory' behind her strategy – she was acting out of timorousness and embarrassment. But it worked. She was safely at her desk, tap-tapping away. Eventually, the self-consciousness gave way to absorption; the mechanical lines to real work.

Frame's opening lines didn't matter at all; Grand's mattered far too much. The portrayal of Grand is exaggerated for satirical effect, of course, but he does show traits and motivations recognisable to many aspiring writers. He is ambitious and eager for success. He is also dogged by a paralysing perfectionism. His soaring ambition and crippled creativity seem to go hand in hand. Ambition and high standards are important, even essential at certain points, but they can obstruct and deaden writers in the production stages of work.

A researcher into creativity, Mihaly Csikszentmihalyi (1996), warned that artists must not start wondering how much their work will sell for or what the critics will think of it, not if they want to 'pursue original avenues'. He found that 'creative achievements depend upon single-minded immersion'. He introduced the concept of 'flow', that state of timeless-seeming happiness and concentration which comes when one's whole attention is absorbed.

Virginia Woolf has described this inspired state memorably:

> I walk making up phrases; sit, contriving scenes; am in short in the thick of the greatest rapture known to me.
>
> (Woolf 1953: 115)

The question for many writers is how to get to the 'rapture' without having to go by way of resistance. Some lucky people never have a problem but many will recognise this scenario:

You sit down to write and then run the gauntlet of self-sabotage: 'must have another coffee/wasn't that the phone ringing/should really check the electricity meter/maybe pop down town briefly/that three for two offer in the bookshop won't last forever/maybe ought to read something just to get the engine going/you'll never be a writer, anyway/who do you think you're kidding . . .'

It may be comforting to know that even the most famous writers can be assailed by doubts and inner saboteurs. Here is Vladimir Nabokov:

> Just when the author sits down to write, 'the monster of grim commonsense' will lumber up the steps to whine that the book is not for the general public, that the book will never – And right then, just before it blurts out the word s, e, double – l, false commonsense must be shot dead.
>
> (quoted in Boyd 1991: 31)

How can we slay these lumbering monsters or at least shut them up? Let's explore some practical strategies commonly used by established writers.

Develop a writing habit

'Excellence is not an act, but a habit.'

Aristotle, quoted in Sher 1999: 8

Think again about Janet Frame's procedures. She established a habit of writing. Some new writers think that the correct thing to do is to wait for inspiration. They fear that if they try to write in a down-to-business mood or at routine times, the writing will not take flight. But inspiration will not reliably hunt you down at the supermarket or even on some idyllic country walk. Even if it did, you would need some practised skills and discipline to make the most of it. Court inspiration; make yourself available. Inspiration comes most often through the habit of work, unexpectedly, in the form of sudden ideas, ways and means, wonderful words and phrases, and sometimes complete breakthroughs. Kenzabura Oë, Nobel prize-winning novelist, said that it is 'accumulated practice' which enables the writer to 'reveal a landscape no one has ever seen before' (quoted in Sher 1999: 16). Writers practise regularly, just as musicians play and artists sketch.

Perhaps you're wondering how you could possibly fit regular writing practice into a busy life? In his essay, 'Fires', Raymond Carver, 1986 [1982] describes a decade of struggle to write while 'working at crap jobs' and raising two children. The essay is about his 'influences' as a writer but he subverts the usual listing of beloved books and revered authors. For him nothing could be more powerful than 'real influence' – the grinding daily responsibilities that obstruct literary work. He describes a Saturday afternoon spent doing several loads of washing in a busy laundromat. He exchanged sharp words with a customer who objected to the number of washers he'd had to use. Then he was waiting with his basketful of damp clothes, ready to pounce on an available dryer. After half an hour, one finally came to a stop and he was right there. But a woman appeared, checked the clothes, found them not dry enough and inserted two more coins. Frustrated to the point of tears, Carver had this revelation:

> At that moment I felt—I knew—that the life I was in was vastly different from the lives of the writers I most admired. I understood writers to be people who didn't spend their Saturdays at the laundromat and every waking hour subject to the needs and caprices of their children. Sure, sure, there've been plenty of writers who have had far more serious impediments to their work, including imprisonment, blindness, the threat of torture or of death in one form or another. But knowing this was no consolation. At that moment—I swear all of this took place there in the laundromat—I could see nothing ahead but years more of this kind of responsibility and perplexity.
>
> (Carver 1986 [1982]: 33)

It can be consoling to know that most writers have to contend with obstacles to their work. Do you identify with any of Carver's difficulties? Or do you have your own problems? Make some notes to yourself about how you might be able to surmount any practical obstacles to your writing.

Can you carve out some time each day, even if it's just half an hour? It's the constancy that counts, the building of a habit, rather than the length of actual time you are able to spend each week.

Include consideration of times when you cannot actually be at your writing desk but can mull over and progress your ideas, or figure out ways of expressing some things. For example: late at night; when you're travelling by bus or train or even while driving (but don't take notes without stopping the car!); in the bath; in the middle of a boring meeting; during lunch breaks at work; in supermarket queues. In this way, you can keep the momentum going between your longer sessions. Start experimenting to find whatever suits you in terms of allocating time.

Experiment also with special rituals and different locations for your writing. Will it help if you play music? Stick inspiring mottoes on your computer or wall? Have a little shrine of favourite books propped on your desk? Where is the best place for you to write? Proust wrote in bed in a cork-lined chamber. Roald Dahl lay on the floor of a garden hut. J. K. Rowling wrote the first 'Harry Potter' in an Edinburgh café. Find out what works for you.

Postpone perfection

The poet Louise Bogan once used the haunting phrase 'the knife of the perfectionist attitude' (quoted in Olsen 1980: 145). Perfectionism can kill writing, cutting it dead as it tries to emerge. There is a time for perfecting writing and it is not at the outset. Remember the hopelessly stalled Joseph Grand.

But what if you find it painful to produce clumsy, ineffective sentences? You should understand that all writers, even the most experienced, can write badly. The gift of writing is a power that flickers – everyone has mediocre days as well as magical ones. Try to cultivate an attitude of curiosity. As Flannery O'Connor said: 'I write to see what I say' (O'Connor 1990 [1971]: ix). Don't expect everything to be fluent or valuable. Virginia Woolf wrote about finding the 'diamonds of the dustheap' in her daily output (Woolf 1953: 7).

Most successful writers have a high tolerance of raw, messy first drafts and of a series of imperfect subsequent drafts. They know that stamina, the ability to stick with a piece of writing until it emerges as the best they can do, is as important as whatever talent they possess.

For example, Canadian writer Alice Munro said in a *Paris Review* interview that she has 'stacks of notebooks that contain this terribly clumsy writing' (Munro 2007 [1994]: 407). She described how she reaches a point in about three quarters of her fiction when she thinks she will abandon the particular story. Days later, she will suddenly see how to write it. But this only happens after she has said, 'No, this isn't going to work, forget it' (Munro 2007 [1994]: 407).

This kind of struggle is typical. One of the most prolific writers alive today, Joyce Carol Oates, is often thought of as an 'effortless' writer because of her vast output: over eighty books including novels, short story collections, poetry and essays. But she says: 'When people accuse me of writing easily, I can't imagine what they mean.' She writes by hand, starting stories countless times, making comments as she goes, often producing as many as a thousand pages of notes for every 250 printed pages (in Arana 2003: 11). The 'secret' of good writing is rewriting.

The most empowering right you can give yourself is the entitlement to write roughly, uncertainly, even badly.

Writing a first draft is like groping your way into a darkened room, or trying to catch a faintly overheard conversation. It is only when you have some kind of scaffolding down on the page that you will begin to glimpse the ultimate shape of your narrative.

Use techniques to free up your writing

The poet Paul Muldoon advises new writers not to think of themselves primarily as writers but as receivers (Open University 2004). The writer acts as a kind of medium or channel, catching the words and organising them. You stay alert and 'listen' instead of bracing yourself for some hard test. If you cultivate an attitude of curiosity, trust, and receptivity towards writing, it will flow more easily.

There are several techniques that can help with this. They are often referred to as methods for 'harnessing the unconscious mind'. The idea is that our conscious mind contains only a fraction of our selves and we need to tap the huge fund of ideas, images, memories and emotions that make up our unconscious minds. All of the methods involve fast unpremeditated writing. This is in order to bypass the intellect or the internal 'censor', which is always trying to evaluate and direct the writing.

Freewriting

In freewriting – a term coined by Peter Elbow – we permit ourselves to associate freely, that is to write down the first words that occur to us, then whatever that makes us think of, following the train of thought wherever it goes. It can feel uncomfortable, especially at first. You may feel that what you are writing is silly or unseemly or banal. You may feel a strong urge to stop or control it. But don't. You will often be surprised, even delighted, by the liveliness and power of the ideas and words that emerge.

The method

How is it done? Let the words tumble out. Write anything at all, what's on your mind, what you notice:

> Like I'm now looking at the tree outside my window. Tangles of dark branches, spooky sometimes, but soon it will just explode into pink blossoms, fantastic pinkness for a few weeks before the wind shakes it all away. The sadness of trees, inherent sadness, but more mournful when there are no trees, like that place in Donegal, rocks and peat forever, no tree outlines against the sky. Remember V. after the stroke pointing at the cactus that had lost its flowers. Look, she said, it brings no more spoons. No more blooms. Her lost language and the new one she puts together and the way it makes sense.

Activity 1.1 Writing

Choose three or four of the following beginnings and freewrite for a few minutes about each one.

- The truth is . . .
- I wish I had said . . .

- I need proof . . .
- I went outside and . . .
- For the first time ever . . .
- It surprised me when . . .
- It was no use pretending . . .
- A long time ago . . .
- I turned the corner, and there, coming towards me was . . .
- That smell reminds me of . . .
- One summer's day . . .

Read over your freewrites. Underline any words, phrases or lines that interest you. Start to build a stock of material for possible development.

Discussion

Freewriting will often take you into your deepest ideas, feelings and memories. It enables you to amass material, some of which can be used and developed in your work. Writing in this way also trains you to be able to write breezily and with confidence as soon as you sit down to do it.

Clustering

Clustering is a technique developed by Gabriele Lusser Rico in her book *Writing the Natural Way* (1983). It is a method based on the distinctive functions of the brain's two hemispheres. The clustering method aims to rouse a generous flow of connected images and ideas and to bypass the ordering, analytical functions of the brain which might constrain writing at the outset.

Traditionally, it was thought that creativity comes from the right side of the brain and analysis from the left. But neuroscientist Antonio Damasio states that creativity requires interaction between both parts of the brain. A creative person needs 'a broad imagination' to produce 'a torrent of material'. Then they must have 'an educated emotional response to this flood of ideas'. Finally, they must have 'a good reasoning process to shape and communicate their ideas to others' (quoted in Wade 2003).

Part of the trick of creativity is being able to move backwards and forwards between different areas of the brain as needed. Often, when we begin to think about writing something, we go into analytical mode, making lists, taking things step by step. Clustering, which is more like drawing or sketching than writing, helps to produce an initial wealth of material, all emotionally suffused, and reaching towards a tentative whole. It can enable us to begin writing more easily and coherently.

The method

To make a cluster, you take a fresh page and choose a word or phrase which represents the subject you wish to write about. For example, you might use single words like 'water', 'fire', 'India', or phrases like 'love at first sight'. Write this nucleus word or phrase in the centre of the page, circle it and then write down every connection that comes into your head. Let the words or phrases fan out from the nucleus like a branch. Circle each new word and join the circles with little lines or arrows. When you seem to exhaust a particular chain of associations, start another branch. When you come up with a very evocative word, you might start a new chain from that.

A cluster gives you a visual map of your thought. It helps you to organise your writing organically rather than sequentially. It can act as a blueprint of a whole poem or prose piece, or you may find most of it dreary but feel intrigued by one strand or one idea that crops up. Clusters are not an end in themselves. Use them to trigger writing. The simplest way is to launch into a 'focused freewrite', that is, one where you choose the subject.

Clusters are wholly personal and may seem partly impenetrable to someone else. In the ice cluster shown in Figure 1, one strand is connected to my mother's stories about her Canadian childhood, the weekly visits of the iceman who delivered blocks of ice for refrigeration on a horse-drawn cart. Another strand has 'splinter in the heart', which I recognise as Graham Greene's observation that writers have a 'splinter of ice in the heart'. The 'sugar frosting' line was the one that grabbed my interest. 'Sugar frosting' reminded me of a certain type of character: effusively friendly yet brittle and cold:

She has a sing-song voice and gushing manner like she's your best friend. But you know nothing about her and daren't ask. Her whole body looks clenched and her eyes are stony. You wonder what's behind the sugar frosting.

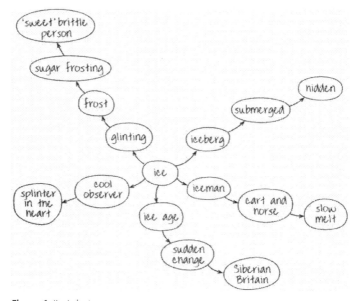

Figure 1 'Ice' cluster

Remember that this kind of freewrite is 'focused' in the sense that you select the subject. You should still write them at a rapid pace, allowing the words to pour out.

It is useful to create clusters for characters in stories or narrative poems. Figure 2 shows a character-cluster I made for a story called 'The Marvellous Boy' (Anderson 1996: 70–89). The grandmother appears only through the memories of two characters in the story but she has a baleful influence. I wanted to get a better sense of her. The cluster gives a portrait of a stern matriarch and the suffocating atmosphere around her. One branch is a list of her favourite admonishments. Sometimes the lines spin into wordplay: 'judging, grudging' and the alliterative 'asthma/ask for nothing', the kind of word design often obtained in clusters.

For me, the surprising leap in the cluster was from 'queen bee' to 'cockroach'. Then 'white cockroach' cropped up after 'whited sepulchre', the Biblical image for a pious hypocrite. I had no idea what these meant

Figure 2 'Grandmother' cluster

when I was doing the cluster. But I remembered later that the queen of a cockroach nest is white and the image fitted the story, which is essentially about an invincible unfeelingness, a numbing of the heart. The white cockroach queen represents that in the story and adds to its symbolic level. Without the cluster, I would never have come up with the idea.

Activity 1.2 Writing

Make four clusters followed by focused freewrites based on what interests you most in your clusters. Spend no more than 3 minutes on each cluster and the same amount of time on each of your freewrites.

Choose your nucleus words from these lists, taking at least one from each:

- Family, friendship, the end of the affair, fame, rivalry, getting older, conflict.
- Afraid, angry, sad, hopeful, forgiving, suspicious, jealous, homesick.
- House, doll, photo album, flowers, gun, shoes, money.

Discussion

Again, underline any parts of your freewrites which you feel you could develop further or use as they stand in a poem or story.

Which kind of nucleus word worked best for you – an object, feeling, or big abstract idea? Did you find yourself anchoring the abstract idea to specific, concrete details? If so, this could be a useful kind of cluster to make when you want to explore 'big' themes, which are best translated into the personal and specific. For example, 'war' is a soldier with post-traumatic stress syndrome; 'neighbourliness' is Marie looking after Sam's dog while he's in hospital.

As well as using clusters at the start of any writing, also try clustering any time you get stuck. When the sentences refuse to march across the page, clusters are much less daunting.

Activity 1.3   Writing

Practise clustering and freewriting for 20 minutes every day for a week. The objective is to begin your 'habit of writing'; become adept at the two techniques; and to turn up possible ideas and material for later use. You can choose your own 'triggering' words, or select from the suggestions below:

For freewriting, choose from these beginnings:

- Coffee, toast and three paracetamol . . .
- She said it might put things in perspective . . .
- I thought he would never change . . .
- There was something unbelievable in the desk drawer . . .
- They didn't even care . . .
- I thought I heard a noise . . .
- I love my new . . .

You can choose clusters from any of these: heartache, spiders, skating on thin ice, fudge, purple, the best time ever, mirror, letting go.

Remember to move into a focused freewrite when you come up with exciting or revealing ideas.

Give yourself patient time

Unlike musicians or artists, who expect to undertake long training and practice, writers often feel impatient and unforgiving of themselves if they cannot swiftly produce accomplished work. This may be because our medium is the language we have already acquired and use incessantly. But it takes a long time to master the crafts of writing, to wrestle our ideas into the best arranged words, to find our special themes or to let them find us. 'Finding a voice', the writer's creation of a distinctive personal style or 'signature', also takes time and confidence to emerge. John Gardner, writing about this issue in connection with fiction writing in particular, thought it best illustrated by an example:

> Notice the careful, tentative quality of the opening paragraph of Melville's *Omoo*:
>
>> It was in the middle of a bright tropical afternoon that we made good our escape from the bay. The vessel we sought lay with her main-topsail aback about a league from the land, and was the only object that broke the broad expanse of the ocean.
>
> There is, I think, nothing actively bad about this writing; but we get no sense of the speaker's character, no clear mood from the rhythm (we cannot tell how seriously to take the word 'escape'), certainly no sense of prose invading the domain of poetry. [. . .]
>
> Compare what the same writer can do once he's found his booming authoritative voice:
>
>> Call me Ishmael. Some years ago – never mind how long precisely – having little or no money in my purse, and nothing particular to interest me on shore, I thought I would sail about a little and see the watery part of the world . . .
>
> (Gardner 1985 [1983]: 66–67)

The implication here is not that writers should necessarily seek a 'booming, authoritative voice'. Your particular voice might be sensuous, oratorical, tender, wisecracking, or whatever expresses you best. The point is that writing is a practice and a process. It requires patient time in abundance.

Avoid writer's block

It seems to be fashionable recently to deny the existence of writer's block. It is sometimes dismissed as a form of malingering; nothing that a bit of brisk determination would not cure. Just don't believe in it, seems to be the message. If it's not one of your articles of faith, then it won't happen to you. And perhaps some writers do talk about it too casually, claiming to be blocked when they are simply jaded or going through a period of silent renewal, that state which Keats called *agonie ennuyeuse* ('tedious agony' quoted in Olsen 1980: 6). In a fallow period, things are still growing out of sight.

But writer's block is a real condition and an oppressive one. Thomas Hardy stopped writing novels twenty-eight years before the end of his life, 'grated to pieces by the constant attrition' (Olsen 1980: 122) of the censorship of his time. Gerard Manley Hopkins, torn between his vocations as both priest and poet, lamented to a friend in 1881 that 'every impulse and spring of art seems to have died in me . . .' (Olsen 1980: 129).

Activity 1.4   Reading

George Gissing's 1891 novel *New Grub Street* (1993) features Edwin Reardon, a writer of talent and high principles, who has enjoyed a modest literary success. He marries a socially ambitious woman, who expects him to achieve fame and money. The novel shows one of the most agonising attacks of writer's block ever described.

- Is there anything surprising to you in this portrayal of writer's block?

For months he had been living in this way; endless circling, perpetual beginning, followed by frustration. A sign of exhaustion, it of course made exhaustion more complete. At times he was on the border-land of imbecility; his mind looked into a cloudy chaos, a shapeless whirl of nothings. He talked aloud to himself, not knowing that he did so. Little phrases which indicated dolorously the subject of his preoccupation often escaped him in the street: 'What could I make of that, now?' 'Well, suppose I made him———?' 'But no, that wouldn't do,' and so on. (. . .)

The ordering of his day was thus. At nine, after breakfast, he sat down to his desk, and worked till one. Then came dinner, followed by a walk. As a rule he could not allow Amy to walk with him, for he had to think over the remainder of the day's toil, and companionship would have been fatal. At about half-past three he again seated himself, and wrote until half-past six, when he had a meal. Then once more to work from half-past seven to ten. Numberless were the experiments he had tried for the day's division. The slightest interruption of the order for the time being put him out of gear; Amy durst not open his door to ask however necessary a question.

Sometimes the three hours' labour of a morning resulted in half-a-dozen lines, corrected into illegibility. His brain would not work; he could not recall the simplest synonyms; intolerable faults of composition drove him mad. He would write a sentence beginning thus: 'She took a book with a look of———;' or thus: 'A revision of this decision would have made him an object of derision.' Or, if the period were otherwise inoffensive, it ran in a rhythmic gallop which was torment to the ear. All this, in spite of the fact that his former books had been noticeably good in style. He had an appreciation of shapely prose which made him scorn himself for the kind of stuff he was now turning out.

(Gissing 1993 [1891]: 123–4)

Discussion

It might be surprising that Edwin Reardon is a published writer, already building a reputation, but this does not protect him from writer's block. Even more surprising perhaps is that this writer's block is so very full of writing. Reardon is at his desk for almost ten hours daily and spurns companionship during his afternoon 'break' so that he can stay focused.

His self-persecution is brilliantly detailed. He moves straight from creation to punitive judgement. He abandons projects as soon as they present any difficulty. He is locked into a system of ferocious self-cancellation:

'What could I make of that, now?' 'Well, suppose I made him —?' 'But no, that wouldn't do,' and so on.

The particular causes of Reardon's plight are that he is fearful of not living up to his wife's expectations. Ambition and obligation rob him of the ability to achieve anything. He cannot write with 'the workhouse clanging' at his 'poet's ear' (Gissing 1993 [1891]: 125).

How should we avoid this kind of calamity? Ted Solotaroff, editor of the *New American Review* for ten years, has written about this in his essay 'Writing In the Cold'. His magazine 'discovered' many new writers during his tenure, about half of whom later 'disappeared'. He speculated that the main thing which sustains writers who stick with it is a 'sense of necessity', a love of writing for its own sake. He quotes the novelist, Lynne Schwartz:

Once I got started I wanted the life of a writer so fiercely that nothing could stop me. I wanted the intensity, the sense of aliveness that came from writing . . . My life is worth living when I've written a good paragraph.

(Solotaroff 1985: 279)

The enjoyment of writing, the pleasures of finding the precise word, of watching a fictional character unfold, of hitting on the right graceful rhythm for a poem: these are *intrinsic* rewards.

The desire for publication or for a good grade or for some stunned admiration from fellow-members of a writers' group – these are *extrinsic* rewards, potentially ensuing from the activity of writing but not part of the experience itself.

Researchers have found that creativity increases when a person's motivation is intrinsic. For example, T.M. Amabile carried out an experiment with seventy-two creative writing students in 1985 (Amabile, 1985). All of the students wrote a poem. Amabile then divided the students into two groups and distributed lists of reasons for writing. One group received a list emphasising intrinsic factors and the other received extrinsic motivations such as: 'You want your writing teachers to be favourably impressed with your writing talent' and 'You know that many of the best jobs available require good writing skills'. The students were then asked to write a second poem. External evaluators rated both poems from each student. Amabile found that there was a significant dip in achievement in the second poems written by students given the extrinsic list. Their writing was actually damaged by a focus on external rewards.

So, it seems best to leave our ambitions and obligations, our dreams and our deadlines, outside the door when we write; that way, we will find ourselves more often in the 'thick of the rapture' of writing.

References

Amabile, T.M. (1985) 'Motivation and Creativity: Effects of motivational orientation on creative writers', *Journal of Personality and Social Psychology*, No.48, pp.393–99.

Anderson, Linda (1996) 'The Marvellous Boy', in Lizz Murphy (ed.) *Wee Girls: Women writing from an Irish perspective*, Australia: Spinifex.

Arana, Marie (ed.) (2003) *The Writing Life: Writers on how they think and work*, New York: Public Affairs.

Boyd, Brian (1991) *Vladimir Nabokov: The American years*, Princeton, N.J.: Princeton University Press.

Camus, Albert (1960 [1947]) *The Plague*, London: Penguin.

Carver, Raymond (1986 [1982]) 'Fires' in *Fires*, London: Picador.

Csikszentmihalyi, Mihaly (1996) *Creativity*, London: HarperCollins.

Frame, Janet (1984) *An Angel at My Table: An autobiography*, Volume 2, London: Women's Press.

Gardner, John (1985 [1983]) *On Becoming A Novelist*, New York: Harper & Row.

Gissing, George (1993 [1891]) *New Grub Street*, Oxford: Oxford University Press.

Lusser Rico, Gabriele (1983) *Writing the Natural Way*, Los Angeles: Tarcher.

Munro, Alice (2007 [1994]) in 'The *Paris Review* Interviews', vol. 2, edited by Philip Gourevitch, Edinburgh: Canongate Books Ltd.

O'Connor, Flannery (1990 [1971]) *The Complete Stories*, introduced by Robert Giroux, London: Faber & Faber.

Olsen, Tillie (1980) *Silences*, London: Virago.

Open University (2004) A171–6 *Start Writing*, Milton Keynes, The Open University.

Sher, Gail (1999) *One Continuous Mistake: Four noble truths for writers*, London: Penguin Arkana.

Solotaroff, Ted (1985) 'Writing In the Cold', *Granta*, No.15.

Wade, Dorothy (2003) 'You Don't Have to be Mad to be Creative . . .', *Sunday Times Magazine*, 30 November.

Woolf, Virginia (1953) *A Writer's Diary*, London: Harcourt.

2

Keeping a writer's notebook

Linda Anderson

In the previous chapter, we saw that Joyce Carol Oates makes voluminous notes in connection with each new work-in-progress and that Alice Munro fills stacks of notebooks as a way of getting deeply into her stories. This is almost universal practice among writers. Notebooks are also useful for writing down new ideas or observations. Writers are habitually on the alert for potential material and your own life – what you see, experience, think, and feel – will provide the principal source.

A notebook is an essential tool for any writer and has several functions. These range from the jotting down of observations while you're out and about to an account of daily events, your rants and raves, ideas for stories, single words, clippings from newspapers, responses to books or poems you've read, notes from research, all kinds of 'gathering'. Your notebook is for you, and it needs to contain whatever helps you or fuels your writing.

The way you organise it is also a matter of personal preference. You may decide to have separate sections, say, for writing exercises; a record of your thoughts and feelings; a section for memories; a section for story or poem ideas and drafts. Or you might like to simply add things in the order they occur, making a kind of creative compost heap. You might like to have one notebook for everything or keep separate ones, for example, a small unobtrusive notebook for carrying around with you and a larger one at home for fuller, more reflective writing.

The practicalities

First you need to think carefully about what sort of notebook will suit you. It will be a companion to you and your writing, and you need to be happy with it. It's up to you whether you prefer small bound notebooks or ones with tear-off pages; a loose-leaf file; sets of index cards; or even a hand-held computer.

Have a browse round a local stationery store. Only buy a beautiful hardback notebook if that would inspire you. If you think you might find it too forbidding to scribble in, choose something else. You need to allow yourself to write in a rapid, impulsive way. Get cheap school exercise books if that would give you the licence to write roughly and to score things out. Choose lined or blank pages according to preference. Remember that you may want to stick things into the book: newspaper cuttings, photographs, or letters. Buy a notebook that you can easily carry around. If you are attracted to an unwieldy one, use that one at home and carry a different one for note-taking outside.

Gathering

In this section we will look in more detail at the sorts of things that might go into your notebook and give you practice in some of them.

Observations of your environment

Carry your notebook wherever you go and get used to jotting down anything that strikes you as interesting: descriptions of people and places, snatches of overheard conversation, sudden insights and ideas. This practice of hopeful, purposeful looking will quickly sharpen your perception. The immediate capturing of your impressions will ensure that you write them when they are 'hot'. The notebook in your pocket or bag will also remind you that you are a writer even when other duties seem to marginalise the activity. You will soon find yourself automatically putting impressions into words. The biographer Michael Holroyd has written about his habit of taking long night-time walks in London as a young man, thinking about 'people, usually, and paragraphs' (Holroyd 2004).

Activity 2.1 Reading and writing

Here is Virginia Woolf's entry in her diary for 4 October 1934, a description of the impact of a storm on her garden pond at Asheham.

> A violent rain storm on the pond. The pond is covered with little white thorns; springing up and down: the pond is bristling with leaping white thorns, like the thorns on a small porcupine; bristles; then black waves; cross it; black shudders; and the little water thorns are white; a helter skelter rain and the elms tossing it up and down; the pond overflowing on one side; lily leaves tugging; the red flower swimming about; one leaf flapping; then completely smooth for a moment; then prickled; thorns like glass; but leaping up and down incessantly; a rapid smirch of shadow. Now light from the sun; green and red; shiny; the pond a sage green; the grass brilliant green; red berries on the hedges; the cows very white; purple over Asheham.

(Woolf 1953: 220)

Notice the urgency of this writing. Woolf is bent on capturing fleeting change and motion and the result is cinematic and exact. The odd punctuation (all those semi-colons) isolates each little change like single snapshots. There is a sense of the writer's scrutiny and headlong excitement in trying to convey the scene 'right here, right now'.

Try this the next time you are outside. Take a few minutes to stare at your surroundings. Focus on weather, movement, colour, and detail. Move from the small details to the larger surroundings as Woolf does – in her scene, she moves gradually outwards from the rain on the pond to the hedges, then to the cows and sky.

Concern yourself with atmosphere and exact pictorial detail rather than correct sentence structure. You are trying to see things in a fresh, immediate way. Spend about 10 minutes on this exercise.

Don't force comparisons but if anything reminds you of something else, write it down. Woolf describes the driving rain as 'thorns' and then compares the thorns to a porcupine's bristles and then to glass.

The search for similes (when something is *like* something else) and metaphors (when something is said to actually *be* something else, for example, 'his violence is a cooled volcano') can enhance writing, making us see things in a new way. Practise seeing likenesses in unlike things and collect possible images, similes and metaphors in your notebook.

Record of daily events

Many writers like to use their notebooks like a traditional diary, recording small events, analyses of relationships, thoughts and feelings, joys and gripes. This can be useful in several ways.

- It can act as a dumping ground for thoughts which might otherwise obsess you and get in the way of writing.
- It can increase your self-understanding. The examination of your own life can also help to deepen your knowledge of the rest of humanity.
- It can be a repository of possible raw material for fiction even if you do not write autobiographically. There is rarely a direct transfer from real life to the page, in any case. As Katherine Anne Porter said, there is always a kind of 'paraphrase' operating when we use real events, places, or people in our work (in Moore 1993: 204).

Somerset Maugham published excerpts from notebooks which he kept from 1892 to 1949, in *A Writer's Notebook*. He explains his single-minded intention in keeping notebooks:

> I never made a note of anything that I did not think would be useful to me at one time or another in my work, and though, especially in the early notebooks, I jotted down all kinds of thoughts and emotions of a personal nature, it was only with the intention of ascribing them sooner or later to the creatures of my invention. I meant my notebooks to be a storehouse of materials for future use.
>
> (Maugham 2001 [1949]: xiv–xv)

He describes a kind of deliberate use of his own experience as a sort of laboratory, a dispassionate raiding of the self. In this way, a writer's private record of his or her own life has a purpose beyond itself.

Activity 2.2   Reading and writing

Maugham's notebooks are full of observations of people and reflections about writing. In an entry written in 1922, he explores the difficulty of portraying contradiction and complexity in fictional characters. He presents the problem in a dramatic way by listing a known woman's appalling faults and surprising virtues.

> Things were easier for the old novelists who saw people all of a piece. Speaking generally, their heroes were good through and through, their villains wholly bad. But take X, for instance. She is not only a liar, she is a mytho-maniac who will invent malicious stories that have no foundation in fact and will tell them so convincingly, with such circumstantial detail, that you are almost persuaded she believes them herself. She is grasping and will hesitate at no dishonesty to get what she wants. She is a snob and will impudently force her acquaintance on persons who she knows wish to avoid it. She is a climber, but with the paltriness of her mind is satisfied with the second rate; the secretaries of great men are her prey, not the great men themselves. She is vindictive, jealous and envious. She is a quarrelsome bully. She is vain, vulgar and ostentatious. There is real badness in her.
>
> She is clever. She has charm. She has exquisite taste. She is generous and will spend her own money, to the last penny, as freely as she will spend other people's. She is hospitable and takes pleasure in the pleasure she gives her guests. Her emotion is easily aroused by a tale of love and she will go out of her way to relieve the distress of persons who mean nothing to her. In sickness she will show herself an admirable and devoted nurse. She is a gay and pleasant talker. Her greatest gift is her capacity for sympathy. She will listen to your troubles with genuine commiseration and with unfeigned kindliness will do everything she can to relieve them or to help you to bear them. She will interest herself in all that concerns you, rejoice with you in your success and take part in the mortifications of your failure. There is real goodness in her.
>
> She is hateful and lovable, covetous and open-handed, cruel and kind, malicious and generous of spirit, egotistic and unselfish. How on earth is a novelist so to combine these incompatible traits as to make the plausible harmony that renders a character credible?
>
> (Maugham 2001 [1949]: 174–5)

Think of someone you know or remember who displays very contradictory traits. Write a description of the person, using Maugham's 'real badness/real goodness' dichotomy or use different co-ordinates, for example: wisdom/stupidity; meanness/generosity; cruelty/kindness; prejudice/tolerance; refinement/vulgarity; beauty/ugliness. Write up to 150 words.

In Chapter 3 you will explore the issue of portraying complexity in characters in more depth. For this activity, simply describe the character conflict rather than show it in action.

Get into the habit of making character sketches or pen-portraits in your notebook. Sometimes you may only want to record a couple of details. Like someone's screeching, theatrical voice or habit of flicking away imaginary dandruff, anything that you might want to lend to one of your invented characters later.

Writing practice

If you read the published notebooks of famous writers, you will find that they often use them as the place where they 'limber up' for writing and where they reflect on their creative process.

For example, Virginia Woolf often reflected about her writing process in her diary. Because the diary did 'not count as writing' (Woolf 1953: 7), she was able to write it in a 'rapid haphazard gallop'. She found that this kind of unpremeditated and casual writing often yielded good 'accidents' and valuable discoveries:

20 January, 1919

Still if it were not written rather faster than the fastest type-writing, if I stopped and took thought, it would never be written at all; and the advantage of the method is that it sweeps up acci-dentally several stray matters which I should exclude if I hesitated, but which are the diamonds of the dustheap.

(Woolf 1953: 7)

Later that same year, she realised that her habit of writing in this way just for herself was good practice, and had carried over into her professional writing and enriched it.

20 April, 1919

It has a slapdash and vigour and sometimes hits an unexpected bull's eye. But what is more to the point is my belief that the habit of writing thus for my own eye only is good practice. It loosens the ligaments. Never mind the misses and the stumbles. Going at such a pace as I do I must make the most direct and instant shots at my object, and thus have to lay hands on words, choose them and shoot them with no more pause than is needed to put my pen in the ink. I believe that during the past year I can trace some increase of ease in my professional writing which I attribute to my casual half hours after tea.

(Woolf 1953: 13)

Ultimately, on 23 February 1926, when she was working on *To the Lighthouse*, she wrote this gleeful entry:

I am now writing as fast and freely as I have written in the whole of my life; more so – 20 times more so – than any novel yet. [. . .] Amusingly, I now invent theories that fertility and fluency are the things: I used to plead for a kind of close, terse effort.

(Woolf 1953: 84)

This bears out the importance of two strategies outlined in Chapter 1: the habit of daily writing ('my casual half hours after tea') and free-writing, the 'rapid haphazard gallop' that can turn up all kinds of surprises by outwitting the internal critic. From Woolf's account, it does much more than just turn over the soil. It can also help to develop fluency and richness in writing.

Morning pages

Dorothea Brande's *Becoming a Writer* is a classic inspirational guide, first published in 1934 and never out of print since. She advocates daily practice of freewriting (although she does not use this phrase), in the mornings as soon as you wake up. Her reasoning is that this is the time when we are still in touch with our dreams and our unconscious minds and can write in a half-reverie. We have not yet moved into the roles and tasks of the day.

Brande's method is a training in effortless writing. Here is my summary of her basic instructions:

- As soon as you wake up in the morning, reach for pen and paper and start writing. Don't do anything else first – no talking, reading, or grabbing a cup of coffee. Take advantage of the semi-trance between sleep and full wakefulness.
- Write anything that comes into your mind: a snatch of dream, a remembered conversation, a moral dilemma. Don't concern yourself with the coherence, importance or literary worth of what you write. Let the words flow.
- Write for as long as you have free time or until you have written yourself out.
- Without re-reading your material, repeat this practice each morning.
- The next stage is to increase your output. When you are able to produce a certain quantity of words without strain, push it further – a few sentences, then a paragraph or two; a few days later, try to double your output.
- Keep the material you have written. Later, you will find valuable and surprising things in these writings but the purpose at the moment is to gain the ability to write spontaneously without self-criticism.

If you want to try this out, it may mean setting the alarm clock for half an hour earlier than usual and persisting for at least three weeks. You may enjoy it enough to go on for longer. Monique Roffey practised morning pages for two years, writing her first novel, *Sun Dog* (2002), during that period.

Part of the method is to be totally unconcerned with the worth of the material you produce. But paradoxically, this is a method that can lead not only to effortless writing but ultimately to better writing. For example, in her essay 'On Keeping a Diary', Nicole Ward Jouve (2001) gives this evidence:

> Some friends of mine, who were not writers, who wrote clumsily or naively in a magazine we edit together, started the practice of writing for twenty minutes every morning on waking. Anything that came into their heads, any which way, without any care for style ... I was doubtful: but I have found that their magazine writing has improved out of all recognition.
>
> (Ward Jouve 2001: 13)

Record of reading

It is hard to imagine a writer who is not also a keen reader. Melvyn Bragg said once that he 'gutted' novels as a preparation for his own writing. Reading is essential nourishment for writers and we get added-value from it. Not just for entertainment and inspiration but to add to our store of possible strategies by studying how writers obtain their effects. Books can be our best teachers. Even flawed or downright badly written material can help us if we diagnose the faults and think of how we might avoid them in our own work.

In 'A Real-Life Education', American novelist Susan Minot discusses the impact of her early writing and reading experiences.

> When I left home for boarding school I began to write on my own—prose poetry, journal writing. It was the first time I had a room of my own, and I found that writing was a way both of being alone and of finding out what was going on inside of my self. Instead of doing homework, I wrote pages of stream-of-consciousness long into the night. [. . .]
>
> It was then that I was also beginning to be overwhelmed by the power of books. There was one moment I do remember when ambition entered into my feelings about writing. It was a spring day, and I was lying on the grass in front of the library in Concord, Mass., where I attended high school, reading William Faulkner's *The Sound and the Fury*. It was a book I had not been assigned but which had intrigued me when I heard some friends, boys from a nearby school, quote the line 'Caddy. She smelled like leaves.' Suddenly in the middle of a passage, the power of the words rose up and whacked me on the forehead. I felt the earth move as if a huge safe were being swiveled open and afterwards felt flushed and stunned as you are after sex. I'd had this reaction before—to other books, and to music and painting, but this time as I stared at the light-green blades of grass in front of me, vibrating, I was aware that it was the writer who had done something to me. And I thought, I'd like to do that to someone back.
>
> (Minot, quoted in Arana 2003: 50)

Activity 2.3   Writing

Think about your own early reading history and write up to 300 words about books that were important to you and why. If you were deprived of books for any reason, write about that and what it meant to you.

Minot traces the beginning of her literary ambition to an ecstatic reading experience when the 'power of the words rose up and whacked [her] on the forehead.'

Can you recall being similarly moved or amazed by something you've read? Write a few lines about the book or poem that affected you. How do you think the writer earned your response? Was it the beauty or truthfulness of the language? A dazzling style? An unexpected revelation or plot development? A deeply sympathetic character? Something else? Spend about 5 minutes trying to pinpoint the elements that made an impact on you.

Discussion

These two short pieces – about your childhood reading and one of your favourite books or poems – can be the start of your keeping a record of your reading. Make notes on the books you read. What works? What doesn't work? Why?

The more you do this, the more searching and purposeful your appraisals of your reading are likely to become. Reading *as a writer*, as an active apprentice or co-traveller, can not only inspire you but can also add to your expertise.

Daily haiku

You might like to try writing a haiku every day. A haiku is a Japanese lyric form which encapsulates a single impression of a natural object or scene in seventeen syllables arranged in three unrhymed lines of five, seven, and five syllables.

Here are two traditional haiku by the seventeenth-century poet, Bashô:

> in the morning dew
> spotted with mud, and how cool –
> Melons on the soil.
>
> (Bashô 2002: 125)

A chestnut falls:
The insects cease their crying
Among the grasses.
(Bashô 2003: 175)

(Notice the slight deviation here: the syllabic count is four–seven–five.)
    And here's a contemporary one by Helen Kenyon:

Cat
Death on velvet paws.
Sleek assassin, razor clawed,
Purring by the fire.
(Kenyon n.d.)

Activity 2.4   Writing

Spend half an hour now practising haiku. You might opt for traditional subjects (scenes in nature or seasonal change) or try to capture moments occurring in urban landscapes.

Focus on painting a picture in words and stick as closely as possible to the five–seven–five syllable structure. Don't exceed the seventeen syllables but you may sometimes make it slightly less. Don't sacrifice sound or sense to force a strict mathematical count. For example, if we add 'down' to 'A chestnut falls' in the second example above, we get the exact count but reduce the grace and drama of the poem.

Composing haiku can be an enjoyable discipline, something that can be practised on the bus home from work, for example. It trains your attention and your ability to capture a moment in a succinct form.

News items

Watch out for newspaper or radio items that intrigue you in some way or which yield powerful images. For example, during the week of writing this chapter, I heard a radio interviewer mention casually the 'obscenity of old age', a phrase which was received matter-of-factly by the writer being questioned. This set me fantasising about a story of a society in which old age is outlawed.

A chilling image from a newspaper article also lodged in my brain, got stored in my notebook, and will find its place in my work in some way. A

33

reporter – investigating the allegation that human hair used in expensive hair extensions is obtained from impoverished Russian women and even from psychiatric patients or from corpses – was shown into a room in a hairdressing salon. This room was full of trays of human hair of every shade.

Activity 2.5   Writing

Spend 5–10 minutes scouring through a newspaper or magazine now, hunting for any likely material, which might include photographs as well as words. Or turn on the radio to a talk station and see if any topic or phrase grabs you. If you find anything evocative or highly charged, put it into your notebook.

Growing

Having experimented with various techniques and exercises, you may have accumulated lots of promising fragments. What should you do with them next? How do you move on to the developing and shaping stages?

Your notebook is a good place not only for initial ideas and sketches but for this elaboration stage of work. For example, let's go back to the pen-portrait you produced in Activity 2.2. You were asked to produce a description, rather than to show that character in action. Now let's release him or her into some action.

Activity 2.6   Writing

Give your character an invented address complete with house number, street, town or city and postcode and write this at the top of a fresh page. Now have him or her write a letter of about 300 words. The letter can be to anyone – a devoted parent, absconding lover, complaining neighbour, a child given away at birth, a member of parliament – you choose. It may be on any topic but it must be based on strong emotion, positive or negative: joy, relief, love, rage, scorn, vengefulness, and so on. Spend 15–20 minutes composing the letter.

Discussion

You have now moved on from a basic character description to a sample of that character's written self-expression, the way he or she composes their voice to make a desired impact. Your letter will also have the germ of a story in it arising from the history (if any) and possible dynamic between the writer and the receiver of the letter.

If you would like to grow this character further, you could try creating other things that he or she writes: a shopping list, a diary entry, a sentimental verse. Or you could start imagining his or her history. What kind of upbringing has contributed to this character's dramatic contradictions? You might start fleshing out the other character, the recipient of the letter. Or dream up possible events or encounters which would challenge your main character.

Your notebook is a good place for this kind of playing and experimentation. Here you can 'interrogate' your writing, try out possible plotlines or verse forms, for example, without feeling that you are committing yourself too soon. The novelist Mary Gordon said: 'A writer uses the journal to try out the new step in front of the mirror' (in Shaughnessy 1993: 17).

Conclusion

Remember that you can use your notebook for all kinds of writing practice, whatever best suits you: freewrites, exercises and experiments, or diary keeping as a repository of raw material. Use your notebook also to jot down those fleeting ideas and apt phrases that occur out of the blue and which might otherwise escape. You can also elaborate on initial ideas, using your notebook to plan ahead or explore possible ways forward.

References

Arana, Marie (ed.) (2003) *The Writing Life: Writers on how they think and work*, New York: Public Affairs.

Bashô (2003) in *Haiku*, Peter Washington (ed.), London: Everyman's Pocket Library.

Bashô (2002) in *Haiku, Poetry Ancient and Modern*, Jackie Hardy (ed.), London: MQ Publications.

35

Brande, Dorothea (1996 [1934]) *Becoming a Writer*, London: Macmillan.

Holroyd, Michael (2004) *Mosaic*, London: Little, Brown.

Kenyon, Helen (n.d.) 'Cat' [online]. Available from: http://www.baradel.demon.co.uk/haiku/index.htm (accessed 22 November 2004).

Maugham, W. Somerset (2001 [1949]) *A Writer's Notebook*, London: Vintage Classic.

Moore, Lorrie (1993) 'Better and Sicker' in Clare Boylan (ed.) *The Agony and the Ego: The art and strategy of fiction writing explored*, London: Penguin.

Roffey, Monique (2002) *Sun Dog*, London: Scribner.

Shaughnessy, Susan (1993) *Meditations for Writers*, London: Aquarian Press/Thorsons.

Ward Jouve, Nicole (2001) 'On Keeping a Diary' in *The Creative Writing Coursebook*, edited by Paul Magrs and Julia Bell, London: Macmillan.

Woolf, Virginia (1953) *A Writer's Diary*, London: Harcourt.

3

Character creation

Linda Anderson

If you have ever wanted to write fiction, chances are that you love to observe people and try to figure out what makes them tick. You're fascinated by their desires, histories and contradictions. But how do we create characters who will seem like living, breathing people, real enough to make our readers care about them?

Building characters is a gradual process. We will usually start with some glimmer of a personality which we need to flesh out. In fact, Elizabeth Bowen thought that the term 'creation of character' could be misleading:

> Characters pre-exist. They are *found*. They reveal themselves slowly – as might fellow-travellers seated opposite one in a very dimly lit railway carriage.
>
> (Bowen 1948, quoted in Allen 1958: 179)

Finding your characters

How might you go about finding characters? There are four main approaches:

1 *Autobiographical method.* In this method you use yourself or aspects of yourself in the creation of character. Whether you want to write characters similar to you or not, don't underestimate yourself

as a source. Everything that you understand or imagine about other people begins with your own experience. Your own consciousness is the only one to which you have direct access. You can create a multitude of characters from it.

2   *Biographical method.* The other main route to understanding people is through observation and intimate knowledge of others. In this method you base characters on people you know or have researched.

3   *Inventing characters from scratch.* You might start with a setting and imagine who would inhabit that place or own those objects. You might build characters from astrological signs or particular professions. Using the question 'What if . . .?' as a prompt, you can start to build details. For example, what if a lawyer only became a lawyer to please her mother? What if she looks like her mother and accentuates it with similar clothes and hairstyle? What does she look like? Start getting the picture.

Or you might remember a stranger's face glimpsed on a bus or some striking portrait in a gallery may have lodged in your mind. You might cut out magazine photographs of faces that move or interest you. I still cherish a photograph which helped me to develop a male character for my first novel, a young school dropout who joins the army. I came across the picture in a magazine one day and thought 'That's him!' The man in the photograph had a complicated look, robust and open-faced but with something more withheld and knowing in the expression of the eyes and set of the mouth. Once I found the picture, my character became embodied, definite. Watch out for this kind of stimulus.

4   *Combination method.* This is the final method and the one most used. You mix aspects of known people with totally invented details. For example, take your own red hair and spendthrift habits, borrow someone else's low-carb diet and family feud, and donate the lot to a shop assistant nagged by stifled ambition. Or take your best friend's deadpan wit, make him handsome but with bad teeth, and turn him into a hopeless romantic who falls in love easily and often.

The combination method avoids some of the fears and pitfalls which can be associated with the autobiographical and biographical methods. If it makes you uncomfortable to base characters too recognisably on yourself or people close to you, then you can select a few features and behavioural styles but package them differently. This kind of reinvention can help to distance you from any stale, memorised feelings you may have about yourself or others.

When mixing and morphing your characters, you can do anything so long as you make it credible, which does not necessarily mean consistent. Although there are certain people who will never run a marathon, visit a nightclub in Bangkok, or own a cat, precisely because of who they are, remember that individuals are highly complicated, full of contradictions and capable of change.

Activity 3.1   Writing

Try out the third method now. Here is a list of ten random items:

- withered poinsettia;
- business card;
- dusty radio;
- silver locket with inscription;
- bottle of herbal medicine;
- auburn hair dye;
- fortune-telling cards;
- jar of sharpened pencils;
- brand new laptop.

Invent a character who owns these things. Write up to 250 words about the character, incorporating some of the objects into your description.

Flat and round characters

E. M. Forster distinguished between flat and round characters in *Aspects of the Novel* (1962 [1927]: 75). A round character is multidimensional, fully realised. A flat character is not rendered with such detail or complexity. These are often background or secondary characters, who sometimes play an instrumental role. They act as 'wheels to the coach', as Henry James expressed it (James 1991 [1881]: 26). But you need to use specific, vivid details about flat characters too, however briefly they appear. Ford Madox Ford taught that you couldn't have a man appearing in a story long enough to sell a newspaper unless you put him there with enough detail to make the reader see him (quoted in O'Connor 1970

39

[1957]: 92). Charles Dickens's novels abound with flat characters such as Uncle Pumblechook in *Great Expectations*: 'a large hard-breathing middle-aged slow man, with a mouth like a fish, dull staring eyes, and sandy hair standing upright on his head, so that he looked as if he had just been all but choked, and had that moment come to' (Dickens 1953 [1861]: 21). Dickens always brings minor characters to life with loving exactitude.

Try to avoid using stereotypes or 'stock' characters even in your secondary characters, for example boring accountant, inarticulate footballer, vain film star, world-weary detective, old-fashioned elderly person, and so on.

Activity 3.2   Writing

Take one of the stereotypes mentioned above or use one of your own. Write a 250 word scene in which you portray that character in a complex way, going against the usual expectations.

Developing your characters

Be specific and particular when imagining your characters. New writers sometimes reach for abstractions and generalities, thinking that this is the way to indicate the wider or universal significance of a particular plight. But the more specific and grounded your stories are, the more they will illuminate the human condition.

To see the difference between the two approaches, let's say that we want to write a story about intergenerational conflict. We'll have a rich, possessive father who has indulged his only daughter. But she starts to forge a different set of values.

> **Example 1**
> He was a 38-year-old, public-school educated man of considerable wealth, who got very upset when his only daughter decided to do voluntary work overseas.

Packed with concise information but who cares? We can't see or feel anything. The characters are mere types. Everything is 'under wraps'.

> **Example 2**
>
> Nigel downed a tumbler of claret very fast. Emily was going to live in some dump of a country full of typhoons and terrorists for two whole years. He marched upstairs and yanked her designer clothes out of the wardrobe, making a mound on the floor. 'Won't need these, then, will you, Princess?' he thought.

Now we have subjectivity, action, and setting. Everything is personal and particular. But this version is more likely to make us feel and think about the implications of parent–child conflict and the impact of wealth than the generalised first example.

Character checklist

What sort of information should you collect about your characters? Some writers use questionnaires or checklists to devise characters in depth. Here are some of the main categories you should consider:

- *Physical/biological* – age, height, size, state of health, assets, flaws, sexuality, gait, voice.
- *Psychological* – intelligence, temperament, happiness/unhappiness, attitudes, self-knowledge, unconscious aspects.
- *Interpersonal/cultural* – family, friends, colleagues, birthplace, education, profession, hobbies, beliefs, values, lifestyle.
- *Personal history* – major events in the life, including the best and the most traumatic.

One of the most powerful ways to identify strongly with a character is to start with the body. Are your characters comfortable or unhappy in their own skins? Are they proud of one of their physical attributes? Do they draw attention to it in some way? Or do they try to conceal some aspect of their body? Do they have any physical difficulties or disabilities? Skin rashes, short-sightedness, a limp, impaired hearing? Think about the effect of any physical vulnerability on their self-image and behaviour.

Think about how a person's history is inscribed on his or her body. Signs of ageing, scars, stretch marks, loss of teeth. The body itself can be a storehouse of memory or a marker of identity. For example, Deirdre

Madden's *One by One in the Darkness* (1996) is a story of three sisters. One of them, Cate, has striven to efface her Irish rural identity in her job as a journalist in London but lives there in a permanent state of home-sickness. Her confident, glamorous exterior masks her deep uncertainties about identity and belonging. As the story opens, Cate is flying home to inform her family that she is pregnant. She is full of trepidation at the prospect of their rebuke. A glance in the mirror at her beautiful appearance fails to soothe her. She touches a tiny, invisible scar at her hairline, legacy of an accident with a hay baler when she was six. Touching this scar restores her sense of who she is, in a way that looking at her reflection does not.

Think about your characters' physical distinctions and the personal meanings invested in them.

Remember the wealth of influences that go into the making of characters. Think about the impact of age, gender, nationality, marital status, work, and religion on them. What is their attitude towards each one of these? Know your characters inside out. What they want, dream about, and fear. Their best and worst memories. How they react to strangers and surprises, to joys and embarrassments. Visualise them strongly – see how they stand, move, shake hands, or eat. Overhear their speech and how this may change in different contexts or moods. The more you know in advance about your characters, the more convincing your eventual stories will be.

Activity 3.3   Notebook work

Over the next week, in your notebook, start creating two or three characters you might use in stories later. Use any or all of the four methods described above to find your characters and then start fleshing them out with as much detail as possible. Work in short bursts of 10–15 minutes.

Credibility and complexity

Conflict is at the heart of stories and comes from within characters and not just between them. People all have desires, traits, and inclinations which are at war with each other. Sometimes the more closely we know people, the harder it becomes to sum them up because we see their contradictions. Think of the high-powered manager who is submissive at home, the person driven by ambition who also likes to vegetate, the lively, funny person with underlying sadness, the confident extrovert who feels secretly shy, the person who lavishes gifts and treats on friends but never leaves a tip, and so on. Aristotle called these conflicts within character 'consistent inconsistencies' (Aristotle 1996: 24). We need to capture these in order to make our characters credible and complex. They are necessary to spark the 'engine' of our stories as it is these contradictions which generate dilemmas or obstacles for the characters to deal with.

Activity 3.4   Writing

Try this exercise which is based on the fact that most people's faces are faintly asymmetrical. Look at people's faces in some place like a doctor's waiting room, supermarket queue or café where you have a chance to study them for a couple of minutes. Be discreet, of course! See each face as two halves and try to detect a different character in each. For example, some pairings that students have found before are: artful dodger/serious student; romantic poet/traffic warden; wise child/partygoer; warrior/playboy; dreamer/disciplined worker; joker/rescuer; practical mother/lone intellectual.

It can also be good to try this method with friends or family members, if you wish to base or partly base your characters on known individuals. But remember that whatever you find may not be 'true'. The point of the exercise is not detective work or uncovering secrets but to build a habit of seeing characters as made up of different, often surprising, component selves.

Take one of the 'dual' characters you have come up with and write up to 250 words of their current thoughts, allowing both aspects to filter through.

Discussion

Here is an example using the 'romantic poet/traffic warden' pairing.

I must be the only traffic warden who uses a gold-nibbed pen to write out these tickets. It's crazy, really – I have to wait for the ink to dry and that gives the irate punters a chance to pounce and tell me how blameless they are. But they know the score. Once issued, these tickets cannot be withdrawn. The most influential things I ever write.

I don't usually care but sometimes I wish I could unwrite them. Like today – that young woman who caught me just as I was placing the ticket. She didn't protest at all, just looked defeated. She was beautiful but frail-looking. Her hair was fine, so fine it looked breakable, like dragonflies' legs. I wondered if that was a good simile. I wondered if she's ill. I walked round the corner and saw something strange. Flowers scattered in the gutter, twelve beheaded irises. I put one of the blooms in my pocket to think about later.

Notice how this character moves gently between his strict and sensitive sides. He is simultaneously tough and tender, practical and dreamy. In your own characterisations, aim for a similar interplay between contradictory aspects. Avoid violent or melodramatic switches, unless your story requires it, for example if you're writing in a horror genre.

Impersonation

> *For is biology destiny? Not for the writer or artist, it isn't.*
> Joyce Carol Oates, quoted in Arana (ed.) 2003

Writers sometimes feel intimidated by the prospect of creating characters unlike themselves, especially in cases where a failed attempt might affront or even seem like a trespass to readers who know better. Can male writers invent convincing female characters? Can women write boys and men? Should a young person try to convey what it's like to be elderly? The answer is 'Yes' every time. Think of James Joyce's Molly Bloom soliloquy (which you will look at in Chapter 6); Pat Barker's portrayals of the impact of war on men; Rick Moody's searing portrayal of the infirmity of age in *Purple America*.

What about trying to imagine characters of a different ethnic origin from ourselves? This can be controversial but may be done successfully, provided that you do know a lot from observation and empathy. For example, Justin Hill spent years as a volunteer worker in small-town China before writing his prize-winning novel *The Drink and Dream Teahouse* (2001), a story full of Chinese characters, male and female, young and old.

In this matter of impersonation, boldness is everything. Writers who think they can imaginatively switch sex or age will probably find the belief self-fulfilling. But how exactly do you go about it?

Writers can learn from some of the methods actors use to help them identify with new characters. For example, the actor Harriet Walter has described a game called 'the hot seat', which is sometimes used in rehearsals. Actors take turns at being interviewed in character. They must answer probing questions like 'Are you satisfied with your job?', 'What are your hopes for your son?' (Walter 2003 [1999]: 102). If they do not already know an answer, they have to reach for it then and there, and this can deepen their discoveries about the character. Walter says that writers could benefit from such a process and it would help to avoid situations where the writer's voice drowns out the character's own, as when a 'simpleton spouts elaborate philosophy' or a writer 'wrenches a character into a U-turn' in order to 'tie up ends' (Walter 2003 [1999]: 103, 104). If you have the opportunity to work with other writers, try playing the hot seat game. Alternatively, you can devise questionnaires and write the answers in your notebook. Or you might try writing a full history of your character as actors do in the Stanislavski Method as a way of identifying closely with them in order to produce a compelling performance. You can try out experiences you have not had and empathise with characters you don't know. With practice, you will be able to enter with conviction into the mind and voice even of characters you dislike or condemn.

For example, in Dostoevsky's *The Brothers Karamazov* Ivan is anguished by the fact of human suffering, especially that of children. He tells his brother Alesha a story about an aristocratic general who stripped a peasant boy naked and hunted him down with hounds who tore the boy to pieces in front of his mother. Ivan repudiates the Christian ideal of forgiveness for such extreme acts. He rejects God's creation because it incorporates unbearable cruelty. Ivan seems so noble and movingly eloquent that it comes as a shock to realise that Dostoevsky hated this type of scientific rationalist and thought him evil. But he was able to put his ego to one side and let the character call the shots.

Author interview

Let's look in detail at a contemporary novelist's approach to the creation of characters including wicked ones. Maggie Gee has written a very wide range of characters. Some are flawed, like the fun-loving but egocentric

Lottie in *Light Years* (2004 [1985]). Some are dangerously disturbed, like Dirk the racist youth in *The White Family* (2002). That novel was considered groundbreaking in its portrayal of racism as something which also devastates the perpetrators. In 2004, I interviewed the author about how she develops her characters.

Here are a couple of questions to think about while you read the following extract from the interview with Maggie Gee.

- How many different methods does she use to draw characters based on herself and her personal history?
- What do you understand by her description of creating characters by using the 'fault-line in yourself'?

Maggie Gee (MG): I don't have any conscious method of finding my characters. All I can say is that when I start I don't know really where they come from. I'm sure a lot of them come from my past and I think the archetypes in *The White Family* are from my own family although the specifics are all different. But there are a lot of incidents that do come from the past. I think there are certain deep structures in the characters that writers make that probably do relate to their own very intimate past. I do tend to believe that all happiness and all suffering are like a series of rooms that open into each other and you go through the door into a room that you know – but that has many doorways through which you see other people having similar feelings that come from different experiences.

Linda Anderson (LA): You've never been afraid to enter any sort of character however different they might be from you and so you've got a huge range of characters, young and old, men and women. What sort of belief about fiction- making does that come out of?

MG: I really think the accidentals of human life, the externals are not really significant compared to the things that are shared. That is my belief and I think fiction allows us to imagine each other.

LA: You've mentioned drawing on memory and personal experience. Do you also use observations of people around you as a basis for characters?

MG: I try not to use people I know because I think it is painful for them.

They can't answer back unless they're fellow writers. But you can transform things so much that people will not recognise themselves and I think that's part of our duty as writers. If we are fiction writers we can invent enough not to hurt other people or to make them feel that their experience has been stolen. I do use myself. In fact, my latest novel *My Cleaner* is really rather uncomfortable. It's about the relationship between a woman and her cleaner and the woman in some ways is like me. I've had to try and look at the ways in which I might make a cleaner uncomfortable or have made a cleaner uncomfortable. If you're going to use other people, you've really got to be prepared to use yourself in quite a ruthless way. It's your best source of material in a sense.

I think you have to use your own experiences of joy and sorrow to find a way into other people's. Of course joy and sorrow are very acceptable emotions but there are less acceptable emotions like hatred or envy or contempt. When you're writing you have to try not to censor yourself. A good writer is dealing with the wildest and freest capacities of their imagination. That doesn't mean that the story as it emerges into the daylight is without moral understanding or without constraint. I mean I hope nothing I've ever written would make a reader crueller. I think that after you've invented these characters another part of yourself comes into play and that part might be the moral part, the compassionate part. I suppose I feel my business with a wicked character is both to make them real and to see why they get like that because I don't believe anyone is born wicked.

LA: I wonder if we could talk about a specific character in this connection – Dirk from *The White Family*. When we are in his head there are signals of his vulnerability at the same time as he is very alarming.

MG: Yes, Dirk is the racist boy in *The White Family*. Dirk was a real problem for me and then suddenly he wasn't. Of course it's easy to invent a racist character in that, certainly where I live in London, I hear that kind of remark all the time – so the explicit source is easy. I know the remarks that Dirk would make, I've heard them, but that's not enough. I had to find a way of thinking Dirk's thoughts. I must be able to, I must have access. I don't want to think of myself as racist but I've certainly made a lot of silly mistakes before I knew many black people, before I'd read much literature by writers of

47

colour, so I've got that level of mistakes and misunderstandings that I have access to. I also have access to the fact that I didn't actually see anybody black until I was twelve and found it quite alarming when I did first see a black person, so there are all those layers of my upbringing that I can use. It's no good feeling so shocked by those parts of myself that I can't use them; I've got to be able to use them.

However, my way into finding it quite easy to write Dirk was by seeing him as both comic and pathetic. I had to do the two things at once. I knew he would be pathetic because I do believe that when people hate it's because they're not loved and Dirk is not loved by his mother, May. May is a sympathetic, intelligent character but she has this mysterious coldness towards her son. She just hasn't got room, he's her last child, she doesn't love him. So I could feel sorry for him. But the breakthrough for me was finding his lack of understanding, his lack of words, his foolish prejudices, as comic and then, as I wrote through him, as I thought through him, I was in a way laughing through him at racist prejudice.

Now it's really no good setting out to state things in novels. I did not set out in this book to say racism is bad – that would be really boring. What you have to do is find a topic about which you are interestingly ambivalent and then explore it through your characters. Through Dirk, I suppose I explored racist parts of myself, things that are transgressive, things that shouldn't be said, and both tried to pity it and to laugh at it. So actually I found it very zestful in the end writing Dirk.

LA: We can use ourselves in a straightforward way but we can also imagine ourselves in unfamiliar ways. When you wrote *Light Years* which features Lottie, this sort of selfish, vain but ultimately rather life-enhancing person, did that come from imagining what it would be like if you could ignore your duties to other people, if you could indulge yourself?

MG: Yes, I think that's a very good point. We are all stuck in our lives to a certain extent but in fiction you're not. You can reinvent yourself. You can think, 'What would I be like if I didn't do that?' And Lottie, this character I adore actually, I'd love to be Lottie, at least for a few weeks. She's beautiful, glamorous, rich and totally selfish. I think one of my central themes has always been selfishness versus selflessness. Lottie is a selfish archetype whereas a character like May, the mother in *The White Family*, is someone who has not been able to carve out enough space or time for herself ever. So it's live, you've got to find your live themes, the ones that are still live for you and the characters who work for you will be the ones, I think, who let you have fun along this fault-line in yourself.

It may seem paradoxical that Maggie Gee has created a huge diversity of characters (there are thirty in her novel *The Flood* (2004)) and yet relies a lot on the autobiographical method described at the beginning of this chapter. As she indicates, there are many ways in which writers can use themselves. Some of these are unconscious as when deep character structures emerge from personal history. There is a deliberate use of self in daring to confront or magnify uncomfortable aspects of one's own character. There is the possibility of playful self-reinvention, exploring what it would be like to cast off certain traits or values. Drawing on the energy of your own internal struggles and yearnings, the 'fault-line in yourself', is another dynamic strategy. Gee's belief that whatever human beings do comes from something that we all share is also an empowering part of her approach.

The autobiographical method of character creation can be the key to characters utterly different from yourself.

Portraying your characters

There are five main methods of portraying characters:

- interpretation;
- appearance;
- action;
- thought;
- speech.

The first two methods rely on evaluation or description of characters. The final three are used to 'stage' characters, to show them directly through their behaviour.

Interpretation

A character may be interpreted by an author or by another character. In authorial interpretation, the writer tells us about the character, summarising or analysing his or her past, background, motives, mistakes, and so on. For example, here is a brief history and character summary of an archaeologist in Michael Ondaatje's *Anil's Ghost*:

> Palipana had not entered the field of archaeology until he was middle-aged. And he had risen in the career not as a result of family contacts but simply because he knew the languages and the techniques of research better than those above him. He was not an easily liked man, he had lost charm somewhere in his youth.
>
> (Ondaatje 2000: 80)

This kind of authorial interpretation can be a useful technique for when you need to condense facts or move the story on quickly.

A character may also be interpreted through the opinions and judgements of other characters. These interpretations provide a double vision, as we judge the judgement of the character who is speaking or thinking about the character in question. We have to decide whether to trust their analysis. For example, Zoë Heller's novel *Notes on a Scandal* (2004 [2003]) is narrated by Barbara Covett, a schoolteacher. Here is her verdict on one of her colleagues:

> Sue is terrifyingly dull. A living anthology of mediocre sentiments. A woman whose idea of an excellent *bon mot* is to sidle up to someone on a hot summer day and bark, excitedly, 'Hot enough for ya?'
>
> (Heller 2004 [2003]: 34)

We learn as much about the narrator from this as we do about Sue. Barbara comes across as spiky, articulate, lethally observant, possibly snobbish.

Appearance

Sometimes writers neglect to convey the physical appearance of characters. They focus on their internal world as that is more 'important'.

But characters can seem like ghosts unless vividly embodied. Physical details also act as an index to a character's psychology and values. In *The Book of Evidence*, by John Banville (2001 [1989]), the character-narrator says: 'This is the only way another creature can be known: on the surface, that's where there is depth' (Banville 2001 [1989]: 62). Physical portrayals do not have to be static bits of information. They can be part of a scene or interaction, as in the following example from Leo Tolstoy's *War and Peace*:

> The princess smiled. She rose with the same unchanging smile with which she had first entered the room – the smile of an acknow-ledged beauty. With a slight rustle of her white ball-dress trimmed with ivy lichen, with a gleam of white shoulders, glossy hair and sparkling diamonds, she made her way between the men who stood back to let her pass; and not looking at any one in particular but smiling on all, as if she were graciously vouchsafing to each the privilege of admiring her beautiful figure, the shapely shoulders, back and bosom – which the fashionable low gown fully displayed – she crossed to Anna Pavlovna's side, the living symbol of festivity. Hélène was so lovely that not only was there no trace of coquetry in her, but on the contrary she even appeared a little apologetic for her unquestionable, all too conquering beauty. She seemed to wish but to be unable to tone down its effect.
>
> (Tolstoy 1957 [1869]: 12)

By showing Hélène in a social context, Tolstoy makes her appearance part of the action. He shows how burdened she is by her beauty. She wears a forced smile and performs as an object of vision, both triumphant and oppressed.

Action

Actions may be habitual behaviours which provide insight into character. A story must also show decisive actions – ones that generate problems, discoveries, and changes.

Thought

The ability to portray a character's thought is one of the assets of fiction. Unlike film or drama where everything must be shown on the outside (unless voiceover or soliloquy are used), fiction can render the characters' mental and emotional processes. You may report a character's thoughts or show them indirectly or directly:

> She was afraid of what the doctor might say.

> Why wouldn't he look up from his prescription pad?

> Oh no, he looks like a hanging judge!

Speech

A character's speech reveals personality and opinions; attitudes and beliefs; educational level; and economic or class background. The task of the fiction writer is to get the right idiom and tempo for each character. Sometimes when a character's voice doesn't ring true, or when all the characters in a story sound the same, it means that the writer hasn't fully carried out the groundwork of getting to know them well enough.

Activity 3.5   Writing

Choose two characters from the following list and develop their voices: a fitness fanatic; a disillusioned nurse; a bored, gifted student; a jovial social climber; a music-loving dentist. Make the voices different in rhythm, sentence-length, vocabulary, and degrees of eloquence. Write two monologues of up to 300 words each.

Discussion

You may have found that you enjoyed creating one voice more than the other or that one came to you more easily. Experimenting with voices is a way of both discovering and extending your range of possibilities as a writer. Always read your monologues (and dialogues) aloud to check whether your characters' voices sound convincing.

Activity 3.6   Reading

The following extracts are from Bernard MacLaverty's *Cal* (1983). Set
in 1975 in Northern Ireland, this novel focuses on a single character
destroyed by overwhelming political forces. Cal has been drawn into the
IRA by local bully-boy Crilly to act as a driver for them. Guilt-stricken,
he wants out. In these extracts we see him taking part reluctantly in a
robbery and bringing the proceeds to the home of the local IRA god-
father, Finbar Skeffington.

In these dialogue-rich pieces, study the way each of the three main
characters speaks. Observe their personal styles and mannerisms. Are
they terse or talkative? Formal or informal? Do they alter their speech
with different people? Study their jokes, silences, and attempts at
persuasion.

Write down in your notebook what you learn about their characters
from what they say and the way they say it.

Extract 1

*Cal has been waiting nervously in the getaway car outside an off-licence
when Crilly reappears with the stolen cash.*

Crilly had been in there two or three minutes. Then suddenly the
door sprang open and in its shutter-instant Cal saw the two women
lying face down on the floor. He stuck the car in first and revved.
Crilly, carrying a Harp polythene bag, thumped his shins and
cursed getting between the two cars at the kerb. He jumped into the
passenger seat. The gun was still in his hand. They were moving
before he had time to shut the door.

'What kept you?' shouted Cal.

'I was like lightning.'

'What did you do to those women?'

'I told them to lie on the floor.'

'Jesus, I thought you'd killed them.'

Trying not to draw attention by squealing the tyres, Cal drove as
fast as he could round the corner and out into the main road.

'It was easy – a cinch,' said Crilly. 'They were shaking in their
fuckin high-heel shoes. Couldn't get the money into the bag quick
enough.' He was laughing, but Cal put it down to nerves. He

leaned forward and noticed the waft of nervous sweat – like onions – from beneath his own coat. He heard Crilly click the legs of his sunglasses shut and put them in his pocket.

'Sink the boot, Cal boy.'

(MacLaverty 1983: 68)

Extract 2

The two men get rid of their weapons and drive to Skeffington's house to deliver the money. He insists that they come in for a drink and to meet his father.

They stood awkwardly in the centre of the room, uneasy about sitting in the white armchairs. The door opened and old Skeffington came in, followed by his son.

'This is my father, Cal. The man I've told you so much about.'

They were all introduced. He was small and bald, but the image of his son. He even had the same facial tic, wrinkling his nose to adjust his glasses. He wore a tweed sports jacket that looked too big for him and Cal could see that the waistband of his trousers was as high as his nipples. The old man nodded during the introductions but said nothing.

Finbar insisted that they all sit down and busied himself getting the drinks. The old man seemed to disappear when he sat in the chair. His son talked incessantly.

'Daddy was just telling me a great story before you came in.' Old Skeffington nodded and smiled faintly. 'About going through the barriers today. The transistor has been fading recently. Whiskey, Cal? Some water? And Daddy was down getting some batteries. He got them outside the security gates in Hanna's, and had to go on into town. What about yourself, Daddy?' His father indicated with an almost closed finger and thumb how much whiskey he wanted. 'And this young Brit frisked him. He says, "What are those?" about the lumps in Daddy's pockets and Daddy says, "Batteries," and, says your man, "Very good. On you go."'

Because he was a Pioneer and used to orange squash, Finbar poured very large whiskeys. They were in Waterford crystal tumblers. He handed the drinks around and poured himself a tonic. Cal was still waiting for the punchline of the story. 'You could have a bomb up your coat and provided you declared it, I think they'd let you through. I'm a teacher, Cal, and I know that in England it is no different. It's all the boys at the runt-end of the school who are going to end up in the Army. The idiots, the psychopaths – the one class of people who *shouldn't* be given a gun.' Finbar sat down on the arm of the sofa with his drink. 'Daddy can spin a great yarn when he gets going.'

The old man smiled and sipped his drink.

'Do you remember the story, Daddy, of Dev in O'Connell Street?' His father nodded again. There was a long silence. 'Or the one about Patsy Gribben?' His father nodded yet again. Finbar turned to the other two. 'Patsy Gribben was this old boy who used to hang around my father's shop. Every day he'd be in betting. But the drink was his real problem. And then one day you decided to trust him, isn't that the way of it, Daddy?' His father agreed that that was the way of it. 'So you gave him – wasn't it a thousand pounds – to put in the bank. Well, Patsy Gribben didn't come back that day. Not surprisingly. This will make you laugh, Cal. He was picked up off the Embankment in Belfast, totally and utterly drunk. And do you know this, the police recovered nine hundred and ninety-seven pounds from his pocket. Poor Patsy.'

Old Skeffington finished his drink and smiled. He began to extricate himself from the chair. Finbar put one hand under his armpit to help him up. His father whispered something to him and then waved goodnight to Cal and Crilly. His son led him out, holding lightly on to his elbow.

'The wit is off to his pit,' said Cal.

'What?' Crilly leaned forward but Skeffington returned almost immediately. Cal looked at the clock and saw that the pubs had closed ten minutes ago.

'He says he's a bit tired tonight,' said Skeffington. 'But hasn't he such a wonderful fund of stories.'

The other two laughed politely. Skeffington slid down on to the seat of the sofa and asked, 'How much was there?'

Cal shrugged. Crilly said that he hadn't counted it.

'Let's do that now then.'

Skeffington poured the contents of the bag on to the table and the others helped him sort the notes into piles. During the silence of counting Cal felt it on the tip of his tongue to say that he had got himself a job but he knew that the next question would be 'Where?' and he did not want to tell them. If Crilly knew that Cal was hanging around Morton's farm he might want to break his legs – not only want to but might well do it. Skeffington might want to do worse. When they had finished counting there was seven hundred and twenty-two pounds. Skeffington congratulated them.

'I think, unofficially, we should slip a few quid of this to Gerry Burns's wife. He has four kids and things must be difficult.'

'What about Peter Fitzsimmons?' asked Crilly.

'His wife works.'

'Fair's fair.'

'O.K., let me think about it.' Skeffington stacked the different denominations of notes one on top of the other and folded them neatly into the bag. 'Well, Cahal, do you feel any better after tonight?'

'No.'

'Do you still want to – refuse to help?'

'I'm afraid so.'

'Not to act – you know – *is* to act.' Crilly looked confused. 'By not doing anything you are helping to keep the Brits here.'

Crilly nodded his head vigorously and said,

'If you're not part of the solution, you're part of the problem.'

'But it all seems so pointless,' said Cal.

Skeffington paused and looked at him. He spoke distinctly, as if addressing one of his primary classes.

'It's like sitting in a chair that squeaks. Eventually they will become so annoyed they'll get up and sit somewhere else.'

'How can you compare blowing somebody's brains out to a squeaking chair?' said Cal.

Skeffington shrugged his shoulders. 'That's the way it will look in a hundred years' time.'

'You have no feelings.'

'How dare you? How presumptuous of you, Cahal. You have no idea what feelings I have.' His voice calmed and he asked, 'Do you know Pearse's poem "Mother"?' Both the young men shook their heads. Skeffington began to recite,

'I do not grudge them: Lord, I do not grudge
My two strong sons that I have seen go out
To break their strength and die, they and a few,
In bloody protest for a glorious thing . . .

'That poem ends, Cahal,
'And yet I have my joy:

My sons were faithful and they fought.

'Unlike you, Cahal.' [. . .]

(MacLaverty 1983: 70–3)

Discussion

Each of the three men has a distinctive style of speech. Although both Cal and Crilly are terse, rarely speaking more than one clipped line at a time, Cal's speech is more emotionally expressive, and more caustic and witty. His speech alters in the different circumstances. During the getaway his words are agitated and appalled. In the meeting with Skeffington he is sardonic and confrontational.

Crilly is a swaggering brute who gets high on violence. He is dim-witted, baffled by any slightly sophisticated utterance, like Cal's punning joke, 'The wit is off to his pit' or Skeffington's paradox, 'Not to act – is to act.' His silence reveals him too. Full of guffawing aggression in the car, he becomes subdued and deferential in schoolmaster Skeffington's presence, speaking only to back him up.

Set against the taciturnity of the other two men, Skeffington's long, self-regarding speeches indicate his sense of higher status. So does his tone: he speaks 'distinctly as if addressing one of his primary classes'. He reveals his father-fixation in his unwittingly comic attempts to present his mute parent as some charismatic figure. He spouts a rhetoric of blood sacrifice and martyrdom. He is sentimental, self-important, bullying, and ruthless.

We learn a great deal about these men from their words: we see who they are and what they stand for.

Dialogue does more than reveal character; it also furthers action. In the extracts from *Cal* we see the beginnings of his mutiny, which will shortly lead to him hiding out on a farm where he finds work. Dialogue is also often haunted by the unspoken – what characters cannot or dare not say. These functions of dialogue will be explored in greater detail in Chapter 7.

Activity 3.7   Writing

Take one of the characters you have been developing in your notebook or one that has emerged from an earlier exercise. Now present him or her in five different ways in one scene. Include, in any order, an *interpretation* of what the character is like; his or her *appearance*; and a combination of *speech*, *thought*, and *action*.

Discussion

Here is an example of the five methods used in one short scene:

> She was a 32-year-old lecturer who liked to be seen with younger men. They soon bored her but she enjoyed the feeling of triumph over her ex-husband, whom she hadn't heard from in three years. *[Interpretation]* No one seemed to find it strange that she wore nightclub clothes to work. It was part of her 'flamboyant' image, along with the abundant jet-black hair and glossy purple lipstick, which always looked freshly applied. *[Appearance]*
>
> Her latest conquest was a student, not something she usually risked, but he was not taking her course. In fact, he told her that he would never enrol for film studies – it was too fashionable, a soft option.
>
> You'll pay for that, she thought, you little know-all. *[Direct thought]*
>
> She tugged his hair playfully. *[Action]* 'I'm sure you're right. I dare say I'll move on to something serious when I grow up.' *[Speech]*

The first two methods 'tell' us briefly about the character's history, personality and appearance. The latter three 'show' her in action and in relation to another character. In Chapter 7, you will explore more about 'showing and telling' and how to decide on the balance between them in particular stories.

Character and plot

It is a good idea to envisage character and plot as interlocking, rather than starting with a plot idea and then adding in characters. See how events emerge naturally from character. In *Letters to a Young Poet*, Rilke wrote 'the future enters into us [. . .] long before it happens' and went on to say 'we will [. . .] gradually learn to realise that that which we call destiny goes forth from within people, not from without into them' (Rilke 1963 [1934]: 65).

This is not to say that what happens to characters is inevitable or predetermined. It is simply that particular characters seek or 'attract' certain events or encounters.

Henry James wrote a lengthy preface for *The Portrait of a Lady*, the story of Isabel Archer, a spirited young woman who gets entrapped in a loveless marriage with a cold-hearted aesthete. James describes in detail the genesis of the novel and the process of its creation. It began with no sense of plot or set of relations or even a situation 'but altogether in the sense of a single character, the character and aspect of a particular engaging young woman' (James 1991 [1881]: 15). He wonders why his grasp of the character was so strong despite the initial lack of context.

> Thus I had my vivid individual – vivid, so strangely, in spite of being still at large, not confined by the conditions, not engaged in the tangle, to which we look for much of the impress that constitutes an identity. If the apparition was still all to be placed how came it to be vivid?
>
> (James 1991 [1881]: 19)

He concludes that the acquisition of such an imaginary figure is not to be retraced. What matters is that he began to see the character 'as bent upon its fate' (James 1991 [1881]: 19). He asked himself: 'Well, what will she *do*?' In response, he seemed to wake up one morning with the full cast of characters surrounding Isabel Archer and so he began to have the 'concrete terms' of his plot (James 1991 [1881]: 25).

It is an approach well worth trying. Start with a strong vision of your main character or characters. Ask then what they will do? Start seeing the kinds of dilemma, challenge, or conflict they might encounter and you will automatically be generating your plot. This may be expressed as a formula:

Character + conflict = plot

Apply this formula to the characters you have been developing in your notebook. Imagine your characters under pressure, forced to take risks or make choices or to stand up for themselves or someone else. What happens? Let the stories unfold.

References

Allen, Walter (ed.) (1958) *Writers on Writing*, London: Phoenix House.

Aristotle (1996) *Poetics*, London: Penguin Classics.

Banville, John (2001 [1989]) *The Book of Evidence* from *Frames Trilogy*, London: Picador.

Dickens, Charles (1953 [1861]) *Great Expectations*, Oxford: Oxford University Press.

Forster, E.M. (1962 [1927]) *Aspects of the Novel*, Middlesex: Penguin Books.

Gee, Maggie (2004 [1985]) *Light Years*, London: Saqi Books.

Gee, Maggie (2002) *The White Family*, London: Saqi Books.

Gee, Maggie (2004) *The Flood*, London: Saqi Books.

Gee, Maggie (2005) *My Cleaner,* London: Saqi Books.

Heller, Zoë (2004 [2003]) *Notes on a Scandal*, London: Penguin.

Hill, Justin (2001) *The Drink and Dream Teahouse*, London: Weidenfeld & Nicolson.

Hind, Angela (producer) (2005) interview, A215 Creative Writing CDI, 'Writing Fiction', Milton Keynes: The Open University/Pier Productions.

James, Henry (1991 [1881]) *The Portrait of a Lady*, Preface, Everyman's Library, London: David Campbell.

MacLaverty, Bernard (1983) *Cal*, London: Jonathan Cape.

Madden, Deirdre (1996) *One by One in the Darkness*, London: Faber and Faber.

O'Connor, Flannery (1970 [1957]) *Mystery and Manners*, Sally and Robert Fitzgerald (eds), New York: Farrar, Straus & Giroux.

Ondaatje, Michael (2000) *Anil's Ghost*, London: Bloomsbury.

Rilke, Rainer Maria (1963 [1934]) *Letters to a Young Poet*, New York: W.W. Norton.

Tolstoy, Leo (1957 [1869]) *War and Peace*, London: Penguin.

Walter, Harriet (2003 [1999]) *Other People's Shoes: Thoughts on acting*, London: Nick Hern Books.

4

Setting

Linda Anderson

Thomas Hardy opened his novel *The Return of the Native* with an entire chapter describing the broody timeless landscape of Egdon Heath (Hardy 1992 [1878]: 3–7). Chapter 2 has the title: 'Humanity Appears upon the Scene, Hand in Hand with Trouble'. Although the opening chapter still has its passionate devotees, many readers nowadays feel a sense of relief when they get to Chapter 2, with its promise of characters in crisis. For them, dwelling on an unpeopled landscape for the length of a whole chapter may seem akin to staring for half an hour at a freeze-frame of the opening shot of a film.

But while lengthy 'still life' descriptions can be tedious, stories can also be boring and unconvincing because of a *lack* of setting. Stories about emotional problems, for example a woman's anger about her childhood, or a man trying to come to terms with his wife's desertion, can come across as case histories if they focus on inward feeling without much external setting. But give us the unwashed cups, the framed photographs on the bedside table, the faint mothball smell in the wardrobe, the shrieks of children playing outside, the colour of the pavement after rain, the forlorn sound of a dog barking in the middle of the night, the strange mood of bleakness and solace induced by an all-night supermarket – the outside makes the inside real. If setting seems to be slowing down your narrative or if it seems dully informative, the problem may be that it is separated from character and action. Give us Humanity and Trouble and Scene together.

Setting and character

One of the most effective ways of revealing character is through details of the spaces they inhabit and the possessions they have chosen. A character's belongings can act as an index to his or her character. For example, here is a description of Alfred Lambert's special chair in the basement of his house in the 'gerontocratic suburb of St Jude', from the opening pages of Jonathan Franzen's *The Corrections*:

> To the west of the Ping-Pong table was Alfred's great blue chair. The chair was overstuffed, vaguely gubernatorial. It was made of leather, but it smelled like the inside of a Lexus. Like something modern and medical and impermeable that you could wipe the smell of death off easily, with a damp cloth, before the next person sat down to die in it. [. . .] [W]hen Alfred retired from the Midland Pacific Railroad, he set about replacing the old cow-smelling black leather armchair in which he watched TV and took his naps. He wanted something really comfortable, of course, but after a lifetime of providing for others he needed more than just comfort: he needed a monument to this need. So he went, alone, to a non-discount furniture store and picked out a chair of permanence. An engineer's chair. A chair so big that even a big man got lost in it; a chair designed to bear up under heavy stress.
>
> (Franzen 2001: 8–9)

At first the description is ironic. The chair is absurdly grand and sinister-smelling. It's like a governor's chair, a vulgar status-symbol. We might start off thinking that Alfred has delusions of grandeur and very bad taste. But then we learn about the huge meaning he has invested in this imposing chair, which is supposed to reward a lifetime's service and self-denial. He does indeed crave status, some compensation for feeling overlooked. We get a glimpse into a whole life through one particular shopping trip. Possessions in themselves can hint at character but it is when we understand what they *mean* to their owner that we get the richest insights.

Activity 4.1 Writing

- In up to 150 words, create a domestic setting for one of the following characters so that we can imagine the absent person vividly: a middle-aged recluse; a heart-throb actor in a television soap; a foster child; a famous poet with writer's block.

- Create a list of five cherished items belonging to the same character. Now consider whether any of these objects could lead to a larger story. For example, is there a significant memory or secret attached to one of them? Is one of them deliberately concealed? Do any of them belong to someone else? Jot down some plot ideas. The objective is to practise seeing possible stories in settings.

Setting and emotion

The description of Alfred's chair is a kind of static character portrayal through setting. The *interaction* of character and setting can reveal character in a dynamic way and can also generate plot. While people may have their innate qualities, they are also the product of particular places. The reverse is also true. Places are the product of people and of people's imaginations. How we see the places in our lives reveals who we are and how we are at any given moment. A supermarket or a field or a church will look and feel very different to you on a day when you have just lost your job as opposed to a day when you've fallen in love.

Activity 4.2   Writing

Invent a character who visits a place of historical interest, one with a strong atmosphere of grief or light-heartedness or positive endeavour, for example a site of war graves, a museum of childhood, the former home of a writer. Or choose your own place.

- Write a 250 word version in which your character feels unwell and is worried about what the symptoms may mean.
- Write a second version in which the same character has just purchased a 'dream' house. Again use up to 250 words.

Discussion

Check your two versions to make sure that the 'same' place changes with the character's mood. If you have chosen an inherently sad place, how does your 'happy' version work out? Or your 'worried' version, if you have a pleasant, positive setting? Have you shown the tension between place and person? Does your 'happy' character feel guilty or dragged down? Or buoyant despite the environment? Is your worried character uplifted or alienated by the cheerful setting?

For instance, imagine a woman visiting the home of the Brontë sisters in Yorkshire. In an anxious mood, she might think: 'How horrible to have that dark graveyard so near the house. I can see it from nearly every window.' In a hopeful mood, she might be enchanted by the Brontë children's tiny books full of their stories in minuscule handwriting. She might think: 'I'll have that – a big sunny place for my children to play and dream in.' Alternatively, her anxious mood could be allayed by the gloom ('They were so much worse off than me'); or her happiness undermined ('They had everything to live for, but look what happened.')

Setting and plot

So, characters may find settings either supportive or oppressive and either response can generate or advance a story. Where they are in tune with an environment, experiencing a sense of well-being or belonging, the writer will often introduce a disruptive element to shatter or test the harmony.

Shattered harmony

For example, Ian McEwan's *Atonement* opens in a big English country house where the Tallis family is gathering on the hottest day in the summer of 1935. Here is Cecilia Tallis, a recent Cambridge graduate, pausing in the doorway of the dining room:

> Dripping coolly onto her sandalled feet, the untidy bunch of rose-bay willow-herb and irises brought her to a better state of mind. The vase she was looking for was on an American cherry-wood table by the French windows which were slightly ajar. Their south-east aspect had permitted parallelograms of morning sunlight to advance across the powder-blue carpet. Her breathing slowed and her desire for a cigarette deepened, but she still hesitated by the door, momentarily held by the perfection of the scene – by the three faded Chesterfields grouped around the almost

new Gothic fireplace in which stood a display of wintry sedge, by the unplayed, untuned harpsichord and the unused rosewood music stands, by the heavy velvet curtains, loosely restrained by an orange and blue tasselled rope, framing a partial view of cloudless sky and the yellow and grey mottled terrace where camomile and feverfew grew between the paving cracks. A set of steps led down to the lawn on whose border Robbie still worked, and which extended to the Triton fountain fifty yards away.

(McEwan 2001: 20)

But this atmosphere of privilege and tranquillity is banished completely by the end of the day. Cecilia's life is changed forever by her younger sister Briony's misinterpretation of a scene she witnesses between Cecilia and her childhood friend, Robbie. Briony will spend the rest of her life trying to atone. The 'timeless, unchanging calm' (McEwan 2001: 19) of the place proves utterly deceptive.

Antagonism

Where there is antagonism between character and place, there is already the potential for a story. For example, in Bernard MacLaverty's *Cal*, which is familiar to you from the previous chapter, Cal and his father Shamie are the only two Catholics living on a Protestant estate. They receive death threats posted through the door warning them to leave or be burnt out. This is Cal entering the enemy territory of his own street.

As he turned into his street he felt the eyes on him. He looked at the ground in front of him and walked. The eyes would be at the curtains or behind a hedge as a man paused in his digging. He could not bear to look up and see the flutter of Union Jacks, and now the red and white cross of the Ulster flag with its red hand. Of late there were more and more of these appearing in the estate. It was a dangerous sign that the Loyalists were getting angry. The flags should all have been down by now because the Twelfth of July was long past. It was sheer cussedness that they were kept up. Even looking at his feet Cal couldn't avoid the repulsion because the kerbstones had been painted alternating red, white, and blue.

(MacLaverty 1983: 9)

Notice that the atmosphere of menace and exclusion is achieved by the focus on particular, concrete details: curtains with imagined watchers lurking behind them, a silent neighbour, fluttering flags, and painted kerbstones.

Activity 4.3   Writing

- Write a 500 word scene in which a character feels trapped in his or her surroundings with no immediate prospect of escape. For example, the setting might be: a boarding school, a package holiday, a relative's house at Christmas, a hated job which is a financial necessity. Show the feelings through the descriptions of the place, not by naming the feelings.
- Imagine a building (or use one you know) which has been changed dramatically but still bears traces of its former use, for example a restaurant that was once a church, a boarding school that used to be a family home, a modern house converted from a barn where animals were kept. Write about a character who, happily or unhappily, cannot stop being aware of the building's history. Use up to 500 words.

Defamiliarising the known

As writers we need to see our usual surroundings with a fresh eye. In Chapter 2 you started practices which are directly useful in the creation of believable fictional settings: noting down observations of your surroundings; aiming for exact imagery. Keep on noting particulars of places you go – the works' canteen, the dentist's waiting room, a vandalised bus shelter, a holiday beach – so that you build up a handy resource of details and atmospheres. When creating your settings be specific. Instead of a flower, make it a bluebell; instead of a car, a battered Renault. Remember always to use all of your senses to recreate the full texture of existence.

Activity 4.4   Reading

For an example of a powerful evocation of place through the senses, read the following extract from P.F. Kluge's *Biggest Elvis* (1996). The narrator is Ward Wiggins, the oldest and fattest of a trio of Elvis Presley impersonators who entertained sailors and bar girls at a US naval base in Olongapo, Philippines in the early nineties.

- In your notebook, write down which senses the narrator uses to describe the setting.
- How do these descriptions convey his emotions about the place?

I can close my eyes this minute and still smell Olongapo, that mix of spilled beer and barbecued meat, of talcum and cologne venting out of barbershop air conditioners, diesel fuel belching out of jeepneys and taxis, and underneath it all, that blend of shit and urine that the hardest rain couldn't wash away, all of this in that hot, heavy Philippines air, fecund, fog-thick stuff that invited you to drink and fornicate and sweat and rot. I can smell it, all of it, and I can miss it too, right now, that and the noises, the sidewalk hustlers, shoeshine boys, sellers of lottery tickets, satay sticks, newspapers, *anything you want Joe*, and the shills outside of night-clubs, *what you want, baby we got it*, country western, hard rock, mud wrestling, foxy boxing, full-body massage, *what you need, baby we got it*, money for honey, honey for money, quick pop, one-night stand, local wife or partner for life, and the sounds that surged out onto the street and into the traffic, horns, mufflers, and all, the music from a dozen different nightclubs, each one a tributary spilling into that great river of noise, sounds from Detroit and Nashville, New York and Chicago, music from every time and everywhere.

Daytime, Olongapo was nothing to look at: tin roofs and rotting wood, metal that rusted and concrete that grew moldy the day after it got poured. Nothing stayed new in Olongapo and nobody stayed young. It was crowded streets and poor, much-pissed-upon trees and if you looked down at the river that separated the town from the base, it was all gray and bubbly and fermented, a black hole of oxygen debt, like someone popped the lid on a septic tank. Beyond, the bay curved off into the distance, toward those brown, dead Zambales mountains, forests long gone, like the hair that falls out of a cancer patient's head once they start the chemo. Daytime in Olongapo was like a movie theater between shows, spilled pop-corn, sticky floors, bad lighting. But at night, it made Manila look like a one-pump town, and especially those nights when the fleet was in and the town opened itself to those thousands of American kids, guilty, guilty, guilty of everything you charged them with and yet—you only had to look at them, six years out of Little League—they were innocent too, clueless and young, the best and worst of all of us, let loose in the greatest liberty port on the planet (. . .)

(Kluge 1996: 4, 5)

Discussion

Wiggins conjures the place first through smell. When he closes his eyes, it is the memory of the overpowering mixture of odours which comes back first; then the sounds, the 'great river of noise'; and finally the sights. His nostalgia for Olongapo is conveyed by his tone of breathless excitement and his vivid use of language. Wiggins is a skilled orator who uses dazzling lists, shocking similes ('forests long gone, like the hair that falls out of a cancer patient's head'), rhythm and rhyme ('*what you want, baby we got it*, country western, hard rock, mud wrestling, foxy boxing, full-body massage, *what you need, baby we got it* . . .'). The narrator's ability to stack up so many specific, richly atmospheric details lets us see and sense Olongapo. We are transported into that shimmering, stinky world.

Unexpected harmony

In *Biggest Elvis*, there is a tension between the seedy decay of the place and Wiggins's intense longing for it, which intrigues the reader. We could call this an example of *unexpected harmony* between character and setting, and this can be an exciting strategy. Think your town is drab and boring? Why not set a magnificent love affair in Dullsville? Or have a charismatic figure move into a soporific place and wake people up, to the delight or consternation of the inhabitants? Or take a generally despised setting and treat it as magical, a site of possibilities for your characters.

For example, *Eureka Street*, by Robert McLiam Wilson (1996), is set in Belfast just before and after the 1994 ceasefire. Wilson subverted conventional portrayals of the city as an immutably traumatised place, recasting it as a site of change and possible redemption. A whole chapter is devoted to a lyrical celebration of nocturnal Belfast.

> Belfast is Rome with more hills; it is Atlantis raised from the sea.
> And from anywhere you stand, from anywhere you look, the
> streets glitter like jewels, like small strings of stars.
>
> (Wilson 1996: 213–14)

Terrible violence still occurs, jolting the main character, Jake Jackson, into experiencing Belfast again as a 'necropolis'. But the novel is packed with love stories.

Or, in *Long Journey through a Small Town*, a novel-in-progress by Patrick Boyden, the setting is a 'Midlands town which epitomises dullness'. The story concerns the friendship between a grumpy man who looks after his invalid mother and a homeless young woman. Here is an extract from the beginning:

> Sunlight, even when dulled by thin cloud, brightens most things. It
> can pick out the subtle blues and greys in roof tiles, bring warmth
> to red brick, and form to chimneys and tower blocks. What it can
> do to buildings of more architectural merit can leave the spectator
> speechless. He may reach for his handkerchief to dab at the tear
> that arrives in the corner of his eye as the neo-Grecian columns
> on a town hall proudly puff themselves out as if to state 'We are
> tall, we are strong, we are timeless. Together we hold the roof
> up. Between our stems, you the people of this town wander,
> buying tickets for concerts. Behind us, you view the culture we
> contain, the visiting exhibition of traditional Dutch farming
> implements, or some sixties pop group, unironically reprising
> their hits with all the style, dignity and edge of a middle-aged man
> playing *Twister*.'
>
> And the sunlight will quizzically touch the golden onion atop
> the mosque, wondering where it came from and what happened to
> the brewery that was there, ooh, just a couple of years ago.
>
> (Boyden n.d.)

This opening dispels the stereotype of banal, rundown city. The narrator is affectionate and whimsical, even imagining the sunlight and the buildings as sentient. The story itself is entirely realistic but the opening primes us to expect promise as well as problems in the characters' situation.

Real or invented places

For every story, you need to decide whether to invent a location or use a real place, either already familiar to you or one that you can research.

One of the advantages of using a real location is that it anchors the story in a believable world. This is particularly effective in crime fiction, where part of the horror comes from frightening events occurring in ordinary places. It is possible to base a story in an identifiable location but make up aspects of it. For example, Ruth Rendell's *Adam and Eve and Pinch Me* is set mainly in Kensal Green in west London. Minty Knox lives there in 'Syringa Road', an invented street. Everything else seems based on real street names and locations.

> The morning was grey, misty, still. There was a queue for the 18 bus so she walked to the dry-cleaners past Fifth and Sixth Avenues, stepping over the joins. Minty had grown up with street names like that and couldn't see anything funny about it but it made Jock laugh. He'd only been in the area a few months and every time he saw the name he'd cast up his eyes, laugh that soundless laugh of his and say 'Fifth Avenue! I don't believe it.'
>
> Admitted, it wasn't a very nice part, but 'run-down' and 'a real slum', which were what Jock called it, were going a bit far. OTT, to use his own expression. To Minty it appeared grey and dreary but familiar, the background of her life for nearly thirty-eight years, for she'd been a baby when Agnes left her with Auntie for 'an hour at the maximum' and never came back. The row of shops ran from Second to First Avenue on the Harrow Road. Two of them had closed and been boarded up or they'd have been vandalised. The Balti takeaway was still there, a bathroom fittings shop, a builder's merchant, a unisex hairdresser and on the corner, Immacue.
>
> (Rendell 2002 [2001]: 12)

Minty Knox also dwells in a surreal world of her own, communing with ghosts. The diligent creation of locality and of the minutiae of her life and routine makes the derailing of her mind more convincing and more sinister.

Familiarising the unknown

Imaginary settings are important for certain types of narrative, for example science fiction or fantasy genres. Such settings are made plausible by embedding the exotic in the familiar. Elves speak English; wizards lose their temper; an outsider lands on a planet peopled by tiny hermaphroditic beings where the two nations are at war: the strange and the recognisable.

For example, Maggie Gee's *The Ice People* is set in the near future when the world is devastated by a new Ice Age. Men and women are segregated and use feathered robots as sexual partners. Europeans become 'the ice people', a mass movement of asylum-seekers clamouring to get into the relative warmth of Africa. The story is told by Saul, a divorced father.

> I sat in our flat like a man of stone and felt the world turning faster and faster. It was true, yes, it was definitely happening, but all of it seemed remote, unreal, I watched them on the screen, great swirls of black ants, crowding the airports, overloading the boats ... They were real people, though they looked like insects but I wasn't one of them. I was a ghost.
>
> (Gee 1999 [1998]: 120)

The story takes familiar tensions, sexual and ethnic, and shows them pushed to a logical extreme by catastrophic conditions. In details like the tables-turned asylum-seeking, it acts as much as a satiric commentary on the present as an apocalyptic vision of the future.

Setting as enclosed world

Institutions and workplaces can provide fascinating settings for fiction. Schools, factories, offices, army barracks, or prisons often operate like little islands with their own rituals, jargons, and systems of sanctions and rewards. Such settings can generate stories by having characters as initiates, power-grabbers, mutineers, victims, and so on.

Activity 4.5   Reading

Jed Mercurio's novel *Bodies*, about a young doctor's experience of working in a hospital, begins with a dramatic sense of entering a separate world 'with its own speed limits and language and even its own weather'.

Study the choice of language, particularly the verbs, as the doctor goes further and further into the hospital environment. What kind of mood is created by this use of language?

1: The Interior

Leaving behind the outside world I turn off the perimeter road and on the First of August I pass under the metal arch of the hospital gates. Ahead towers of concrete and glass carve blocks out of cloudless blue sky under which I'm swallowed into a city within a city with its own speed limits and language and even its own weather.

As I enter the building my reflection slithers over panes of glass. Windows reframe the sky into blue squares while my heels click on hard flat floors and echo off corridor walls. The air turns dry and sterile and as I burrow deeper into the hospital it cools to a constant twenty-one Celsius. Sunshine fades to a trickle then in its place humming strip lights burn.

Bracketed to a high white wall a sign throws down directions for wards and departments. Each destination is coded a colour and a line of that colour is etched into the floor and it maps the route ahead.

Standing here under the sign looking lost I look like what I am. I slip into my white coat, the same one I wore in finals but with a new badge that puts 'Dr' in front of my name, and with the white coat stiff like armour I plunge farther into the hospital.

Some people ask me the way to Pharmacy. I think I might be able to remember from the sign but I can't and I blush and I have to shake my head.

I say, 'It's my first day.'

They laugh. It's a nervous laugh. If a doctor doesn't know the way round his own hospital then maybe there are other things he doesn't know.

Ahead of me a straight white corridor drops away to a set of doors and through the glass of the doors I see another straight white corridor stretching to another set of doors. In the glass of those second doors I make out a third straight white corridor and all together the corridors and the doors are an ever diminishing series of arrows pointing me deeper in and I feel like I'm falling.

I'm falling through layers of brick, concrete and glass. In the weatherless vaults of corridors and stairwells outsiders dwindle. Here come only the sick, those who love them and those who look after them. From the perimeter road I've travelled inwards three-quarters of a mile. This is the interior.

(Mercurio 2003: 5, 6)

Discussion

The doctor's entry into the hospital is hurtling, almost hallucinatory. He is 'swallowed into' the place; his reflection 'slithers' over the panes. He 'plunges farther', and then is 'pointed deeper' into the multiplying straight, white corridors until he feels as if he is 'falling'. He is almost like an initiate being entombed in an underworld – a strip-lit, dazzlingly white underworld.

The mood is one of foreboding. We expect bad things. The rest of the novel shows how the character does 'fall' – into exhaustion and shame in the pitiless world of the hospital.

Activity 4.6 Writing

- Ask a relative or friend to describe his or her workplace to you, including any machines, special furniture or equipment used. Incorporate some of the details into a scene in which a character is tired of the same job and longs to leave it. Don't overload your piece with what you have learned – use just enough to give an authentic atmosphere: for example, the look of the post office sorting room at 4 am; the sounds of ailing rodents and Rottweilers in the vet's waiting room. Use up to 500 words.
- Write a story or beginning of a story about a new employee on his or her first day in a job. Show the character's response to the work environment and how much he or she is able to glean about the 'rules', hierarchies, how to fit in and become accepted. Give us a sense of whether the character will succeed in fitting in. Use up to 1000 words.

Setting as symbolic power

Sometimes setting can be more than backdrop to action or site of inter-action between characters and place. It can take on symbolic power and act as a dynamic force in the story. For example, in Alex Garland's *The Beach* (1997 [1996]), a secret beach is a legend among young back-packers in Asia, who are lured by rumours of a select community living in an earthly paradise. The story enacts a modern-day 'fall', an expulsion from Eden.

Author interview

Because Andrew Greig's novels are distinguished by their strong evocations of place and time, I interviewed him for an Open University course about what research means to him and how he creates a bridge between research and fiction. We discussed *In Another Light* (2004), which is set on the very different islands of Orkney and Penang. The novel is an example of setting used as symbolic power as both islands are places of a bounded intensity that impact upon the protagonists in healing or disruptive ways. From his home on Orkney, Eddie is recuperating from a near-fatal brain illness. The story follows his quest to find out more about his father, who worked as a doctor in a maternity hospital in Penang during the 1930s.

We also discussed Greig's bestselling novel, *That Summer* (2000), which is set at the time of the Battle of Britain and deals mainly with the impact of the war upon a young couple, Stella, who works as a radar operator, and Len, who is a fighter pilot.

Activity 4.7 Reading

Consider these questions as you read extracts from the interview:

- What do you think Andrew Greig means by his phrase 'sympathetic magic'?
- What does he mean by his statement, 'The past is always present'?
- What methods does he use to make his settings 'real'?

Linda Anderson (LA): I wonder if we can talk first about *That Summer*, your evocation of the Battle of Britain and its impact on two characters in particular. There is this statement in the novel that 'something in the air, in the flavour of the times and people's minds is lost to us' and yet the whole story challenges that notion because you really do set out to evoke what that period was like. Can you talk about the methods you used to do that and the research that you carried out?

Andrew Greig (AG): With *That Summer*, it helped that it's just within living memory. My mother and father were alive then. My mother's still alive and I had her journals that she kept during the first part of the war. I found that incredibly useful because a lot of the little details of ordinary life were in them and one of the big things that came out of it is that in the past things are always present. That is hugely important. You always think the past is in black and white but it's not. As my mum said, we didn't know who was going to win the war, so when you're writing about something as well known as the Battle of Britain, it's helpful to remember that it was not called the Battle of the Britain at the time. They didn't call it anything apart from 'what's going on'. In my mother's notebook I found entries like 'Lamb chops for dinner. Dennis phoned late. Worried about my Milton essay. Czechoslovakia going very badly' and then 'We're at war, I don't know what will happen next. I am three days late with my essay.' That's what it's like during these kinds of dramatic events. People still have the minute local details, their lives going on.

I found that very helpful, so I plugged into my mother's personal reminiscences, her journal, a few photos. There's a coat of my father's which he bought during the war, a heavy black wool coat. I still wear it in winter and I found sometimes when I was writing this book I would put it on and walk out. I just found putting on my father and the smell of that coat – it's an act of sympathetic magic you are trying to perform. That's what I think. To me it's not so much a technique, it's an act of sympathetic magic and I find having objects around me when I am doing that sympathetic magic really helps, so in my shed I have photographs, almost a story board, any little items. I had a brooch of my mother's, for instance, her journals, her letters from her fiancé who was killed in North Africa, a picture of my mum at that age, just around me and I found that really helped me get to that place and stay there and then basically make it up from there. That's the kind of research I do.

LA: But the way you've got the jargons and slangs to do with the characters' jobs, did that come from traditional research?

AG: I think some of it did. I went to one of these war RAF recreation stations and that's where I got the radio direction finding, the whole apparatus for that. There are a lot of books about fighter pilots in the Second World War. The problem with them is trying to cut through the kind of received image we have of it to something that feels more immediate and real. It was only when I read a tiny little footnote that mentioned that the sergeants' mess was bombed as opposed to the officers' mess. These people were fighting alongside each other but they had different messes! I had no idea that that was the case. And then I read that a quarter of the fighter pilots in the Battle of Britain were not British at all, in fact the most successful ones, eight out of ten of them, were not British. They were Irish, South African, New Zealanders, Australian and above all, Czech and Polish. I met by chance a woman who was doing her PhD on 'Poles in Sheffield' and she had quite a lot of information about people who were in the forces who had come from Poland to fight for the British. Then I discovered a book about the Polish pilots called *The Forgotten Few*.

So it started off with somebody I met and then it followed through to a book. When I had that, I knew I was burning to write about these people because it fitted the purpose of the book which was to produce something from a fresh angle. When you're really involved in a book everything seems to come your way; everything is offering you help and if you're open to that, chance conversations can take you to something that you really need to know.

LA: What about *In Another Light* – did you visit Penang? How did you get a sense of what it was like in the thirties?

AG: That was the hardest bit of a book I've ever written because, yes, it's a place I didn't know and a time I didn't know and it was outside living memory. So I had some objects, as usual – I had these things that my father left to me and which I use in the book. A Chinese Buddha, a single domino and some picture postcards that he'd taken and a billiards trophy, and these became my talismanic, almost magical objects. Then I went to the central newspaper library and spent three days reading microfiches of the 'Penang Gazette' for those dates, just to get a feel of the time and what people were talking about. Then I went to the Colonial Records office and got first-hand documents about the various political and military shenanigans that were going on. Then I went to Penang just for ten days.

One of the discoveries I made when I went to Penang was what it's like to sweat all the time, to be drowning in your body juices. It took people usually about six months to acclimatise so when my character first went there, that was what I knew he'd be overwhelmingly aware of. The fact it was seventy years ago made no difference. People always feel hungry and tired and enjoy eating and drinking and cooling down and washing. I've always believed in bodily existence as a way in to imagining characters.

What I do when I go off to a place like that, I'm looking for somewhere that will really talk to me. There was a place called The Crag Hotel, they've got this funicular railway, which opened about a year before my father got there and before the character I'm basing on my father, got there. You go up to the top of Crag Hill. It's three thousand feet up, it's so much cooler, it's lovely and there are all these little discreet bungalows and I thought 'I *know* stuff went on up there'. I felt my father very close to me at that time. I knew that was going to be part of what I'd use in the book. So there are moments when the past of a place breaks through and that's what it felt like. Like at the Botanical Gardens, the same thing: I was there and I had this very odd feeling – I looked up and there was my wife crouched down across this pond but it wasn't her for a moment that I saw. It was the woman in the book and I knew something had happened between the two characters at this place.

LA: In that book settings are extremely important. These contrasting islands of Orkney and Penang seem full of symbolic significance.

AG: Yes. I suppose that all settings have symbolic or metaphorical tendencies for me. I'm fascinated by tidal islands and in fact there are two tidal islands in Orkney and of course I use that: the way something is accessible sometimes and not at others; knowing we are accessible to each other at times and not at others. What I've noticed about Orkney and Penang is that in islands things come back to you much more quickly. Islands are finite, they're bounded; people don't just drive into them and out of them again because you can only arrive one way. As a character remarks in the book, what it's like is you get almost instant Karma. Anything you say is going to come back to you; there are virtually no secrets on small islands. Everything is seen, reported, exaggerated, made up. There are qualities about islands that really suited me to write about because it's a close situation which ups the ante of just about everything. If you ever tell a small fib or are rude to somebody, they always turn out to be somebody else's cousin, you know. You have to be careful what you say and do. There are always consequences and I think novels rely on this notion of consequences.

LA: After Eddie recovers from illness, his interior mind has altered. Could we call that also an aspect of setting because it's the interior landscape and it's changed, he's changed and so therefore the way he observes things is different?

AG: I think that's very true. When you're trying to do a character, even in the third person, the details that you give of what's around them by implication are the details of what they notice. Hemingway is great on this. He just gives you these things – he doesn't say that someone thought this or he noticed that. He just shows you things and what he shows you is so indicative of the state of consciousness of that person. In my novel, Eddie always notices things to do with death. It's not that Orkney's obsessed with death, it's just Eddie's obsessed with death so he finds little death notices in the baker's shop. It's an old-fashioned place where they still put the death notices around the whole town because everybody knows these people. This is about selective detail again and selective detail in this case reveals character or outlook. Place and character inter-penetrate all the time. I think that's the key. You're not doing an objective setting which you describe at length and then having done that, you just plonk the characters and tell us what they're thinking and feeling.

LA: Going back to *That Summer* – almost every line of the book has got that heightened sense of reality and the importance of living that comes from the carnage all around and the constant terrible risk.

AG: It's interesting because that makes me think of the problems I had trying to write the combat scenes, the flying scenes. I've never flown a plane in my life and I've certainly not flown in combat! But what you do is you find something of yours that's equivalent and I used to do this rather frightening rock and ice climbing and I remembered that extraordinary sense of immediacy of being alive, of alternating terror, relief and exhilaration that came from climbing; the way that time slows and then goes very fast. I just translated that emotional psychological thing that I did know about into that situation. So I think there are many professions or situations that you cannot have experienced yourself but you find an equivalent that you feel translates.

LA: One of the ways in which you have made *That Summer* extremely vivid and raw is by using the present tense. Did that help you to feel that it was happening now?

AG: Yes, my watchword is that the past is always present. That is to say that for the people there it is happening now. So I find writing in the present tense for things set in the past is a very good way to stop you unconsciously distancing it.

   I read, when I was starting to do *That Summer*, this thing in 'The New Scientist' and I've never forgotten it. Apparently there are some radio signals that have got caught between the earth and what's called the Heavyside layer and they bounce back and forward. They don't decay; they don't go out into outer space and disappear. They're still there bouncing around, so occasionally even now radio hams pick up the messages between the pilots of the Second World War and the base. You can actually hear them late at night by pure fluke accident. To me that is what writing about the past is. It's about tuning in and picking up the few signals that haven't decayed. It's finding the bit of it that's still here.

Andrew Greig's 'sympathetic magic' approach to reconstructing the past overturns the notion of research as a steady accumulation of facts that are woven into a story to create authenticity. Through the use of personal witness accounts, evocative objects, photographs, and surprising details, he enables himself to enter a period of time or an unfamiliar landscape in the most enlivened and imaginative ways. His realisation that the past is the present for his characters prevents distancing. Use of the present tense can assist this although it may not always be what you want for a particular story. There is a strong link between his beliefs and those of Maggie Gee. Both authors draw on the commonality of human beings despite what may seem dramatic differences at times. Andrew Greig began with the constancy of human physiology to imagine Eddie's father's experience in Penang. Even if seventy years earlier, the impact of soaring heat and humidity on a newcomer's body would be the same as now.

In his discussion of 'translating' his mountaineering experiences to help him write combat scenes, Greig shows that use of your own experience does not always have to be straightforward. If you need to describe something unfamiliar, you can search your experience for a plausible equivalent and draw on that. For example, some writers have used their knowledge of the disciplines and processes of the writing life itself to invent characters involved in other arts such as music or painting. Think about your job or profession, your sports, hobbies and other experiences and see whether you could use any of them as a way into imagining unfamiliar activities that your characters might undertake.

Conclusion

Stories are set in a particular time as well as in particular places. As Greig has shown, research entails finding those poignant objects or intriguing details that will rouse your imagination and allow your mind to stay saturated in the right atmosphere.

Research is also sometimes necessary to enlarge your view even of the period of your own life story or of your own home town. Forget that you 'know' your local area. Investigate it; find out the exact smell of the pavements after rain; how many stars you can see at night. Take walks; take notes. When you travel, consider taking photographs too. For the novel I'm currently working on, I've taken about a hundred photographs in Barcelona. They include a picture of two elderly women sitting in front of a café with their ancient dogs perched on their laps. Another is of a child in a confirmation dress standing on a park bench, her whole figure haloed and blurred in fierce sunlight. I also have pictures of isolated details: areas of pavement, graffiti tags, and market stall displays.

Even if you choose an imaginary setting for a science fiction story, you will need to realise it all in intense detail: its climate, laws, customs, cuisine, and so on. Whether you write about your own backyard or some outpost of the galaxy, make it real.

References

Boyden, Patrick (no date) *Long Journey through a Small Town*, manuscript (unpublished).

Franzen, Jonathan (2001) *The Corrections*, London: Fourth Estate.

Garland, Alex (1997 [1996]) *The Beach*, London: Penguin Books.

Gee, Maggie (1999 [1998]) *The Ice People*, London: Richard Cohen Books.

Greig, Andrew (2000) *That Summer*, London: Faber & Faber.

Greig, Andrew (2004) *In Another Light*, London: Weidenfeld & Nicolson.

Hardy, Thomas (1992 [1878]) *The Return of the Native*, Everyman's Library, London: David Campbell.

Hind, Angela (producer) (2005) interview, A215 Creative Writing CD1, 'Writing Fiction', Milton Keynes: The Open University/Pier Productions.

Kluge, P.F. (1996) *Biggest Elvis*, London: Vintage.

MacLaverty, Bernard (1983) *Cal*, London: Jonathan Cape.

McEwan, Ian (2001) *Atonement*, London: Jonathan Cape.

Mercurio, Jed (2003) *Bodies*, London: Vintage.

Rendell, Ruth (2002 [2001]) *Adam and Eve and Pinch Me*, London: Arrow.

Wilson, Robert McLiam (1996) *Eureka Street*, London: Secker & Warburg.

Zamoyski, Adam (2004 [1995]) *The Forgotten Few: The Polish Air Force in World War II*, Leo Cooper Ltd.

5

Point of view: trying on voices

Linda Anderson

Every story is told from a point of view, the perspective of a particular narrator. With each new piece of fiction that you write, you need to ask yourself early on: whose story is it? Who will tell it? Should the story be told by the main character? Or by a secondary character who witnesses the events? Should it be told by an anonymous witness who presents the action without comment? Or by an all-knowing power who can reveal the innermost thoughts and feelings of all the characters?

Choosing a point of view for a particular story can be a matter of 'intuition'. Perhaps you overhear a character's voice in your head and follow that. Or one character's connection to the story will appeal to you more than another's. But it is important to know what the choices are, what each one requires, and what are the advantages and limitations of each choice. Mastery of the basic techniques you can use to establish point of view is one of the most empowering things a fiction writer can learn. It gives you a range of possibilities to select from and increases your versatility and clarity as a writer.

Activity 5.1   Reading

To experience the impact of point of view, let's first look at two possible beginnings of the 'same' story. Jot down your impressions and responses to each version and think about the following questions:

- Who do you think is telling the story in each?
- To whom?
- How much does the teller know?

Version 1

My father says that our house is like a mini-industrial estate, what with all the cooking, laundering, violin-playing, pet-grooming (two tabbies and a Jack Russell), and the uproar of begging for the bathroom as we struggle to get to our busy-bee schedules outside the home. We all have 'schedules', even me, the 'baby' of the family. I'll be fourteen soon but there will be no amnesty. I'll probably be Baby when I'm thirty years old. Baby Middleton with her high heels, pink Porsche, and job on the twenty-fifth floor. A disappointment to her parents, who want me to be a moneybags all right but a doctor, lawyer, scientist, you get the picture. First, though, they're going to have to be disappointed by my eldest brother, Simon, when they get around to noticing. He has managed to fit some class A drugs into his schedule. I don't know where he gets the money but he sneaks out lots of times after everyone's in bed. Shows up at breakfast staring like a sleepwalker and nobody says a word.

Version 2

The Middleton family are the envy of their neighbours and friends. There are five offspring, all good-looking and 'gifted' in one way or another, and long-married parents who still send each other valentine cards. Susannah Middleton, the mother, runs the household with faultless organisation. No medical appointment is ever missed, no dry-cleaning abandoned and there is never a gap in the supply of teabags, bread, or shampoo. Her system of automatic replacement even extends to the household pets. When one of the animals exhausts its natural span, she buys a new puppy or kitten a few days later. This is not a sign of heartlessness, more like the opposite, a desire to fix everything, even sorrow.

In years to come, she will look back on this time and wish that she had paused to notice what was happening to her eldest boy.

These two openings are roughly the same length and deal with the same fictional material: a large, apparently happy and successful family in which the eldest son is secretly in trouble. Similar details are observed in each account: the zealous organisation of the household, the existence of pets, the value placed on achievement, the parents' 'blind spot' about impending trouble.

But the contrasting points of view or angles of vision produce startlingly different versions.

In the first version, I have written a first-person narration (an 'I' tells the story). The narrator is the 14-year-old youngest daughter of the family. The unmediated voice creates a vivid sense of intimacy. There is a direct address to the reader, who is seen as a kind of confidant ('. . . you get the picture'). We see through the girl's eyes and interpretations, getting an immediate impression of her character and her predicament on several levels: as an adolescent casting off her parents' values; as the youngest member in the family hierarchy; and as the only person aware of her brother's clandestine life. The silence and deception at the heart of this bustling little tribe come across worryingly, creating immediate suspense.

In the second version, I have adopted an omniscient (all-knowing) point of view, which uses the third person (using 'he', 'she', or 'they'). In this omniscient persona, my narrator knows what is happening now, what has happened in the past and what will happen in the future. She or he can make judgements about character which the characters themselves may be unaware of ('This was not a sign of heartlessness . . .').

The fictionality of the second version is more obvious than in the first one, which aims to seem like a 'real' confessional voice. In the second version, we are aware of the narrator presiding over the story and controlling its telling. The language in this version is more formal and dispassionate. Whereas the first voice draws us in and confides in us, this voice is distant and authoritative, almost godlike. There is a faintly ironic tone in certain phrases which may reveal the narrator's attitude. For example, the quotation marks placed around 'gifted' seem to distance the narrator from this verdict. And why say 'exhausts its natural span' instead of 'dies'? Maybe the narrator is hinting at an evasive style of thought in the mother, an inability to face hard facts?

I'm the author of both these versions but my narrators have made-up voices. They may each have traces of my personal voice but their voices are invented for the purpose of the story. Jack Hodgins, in *A Passion for Narrative*, called the writer's own inescapable voice his 'voice-print' and the narrators he takes on, his 'voice-masks' (Hodgins 1994 [1993]: 193). With practice, it is possible to become a different sort of narrator every time, to try on many masks.

These methods of telling the story are just two possibilities among many. We will now look in detail at the main strategies used in first-person narrations. Chapter 6 will go on to explore third-person and second-person narrations.

First-person narration

A story is told in the first person when it is narrated by one of the characters. (An 'I' tells his or her own story.) The narrator may be the protagonist or central narrator, the person whose desires and decisions impel the action, and it is important to indicate this status quickly. For example, *The Butcher Boy* by Patrick McCabe opens with the vivid, disturbing voice of Francie O'Hagan:

> When I was a young lad twenty or thirty or forty years ago I lived in a small town where they were all after me on account of what I done on Mrs Nugent.
>
> (McCabe 1993 [1992]: 1)

A first-person narrator may alternatively be a witness or peripheral narrator, who observes the fortunes of a central character. We see and understand that person through the filter of the witness's view and the impact upon him or her. A recent example is Philip Roth's *The Human Stain*, the story of the downfall of a university professor persecuted for alleged racism. It is his neighbour who tells the story of the professor's destruction and the narrator's status as witness is made clear from the opening lines:

> It was in the summer of 1998 that my neighbour Coleman Silk – who, before retiring two years earlier, had been a classics professor at nearby Athena College for some twenty-odd years as well as serving for sixteen more as the dean of faculty – confided to me

that, at the age of seventy-one, he was having an affair with a thirty-four-year-old cleaning woman who worked down at the college.

(Roth 2001 [2000]: 1)

Activity 5.2   Writing

- Going back to the scenario of the Middleton family, write another opening of that story from the point of view of the eldest son, Simon, in his private journal. Make sure he sounds different from his sister and that his writing comes across as for his eyes only. You might want to include some slang, jargon or abbreviations to make the voice authentic.
- Then write another opening from a witness's point of view, for example a concerned schoolteacher or a nosy neighbour. Use up to 180–200 words for each version, as in the original examples.

Advantages of first-person narration

First-person narration is the most straightforward storytelling technique. It has maximum subjectivity and passion and can therefore be compelling. Access to the character's thoughts is smooth and immediate, without the filter of another narrating voice. You are free to create strongly authentic voices, using slang, faulty grammar, and colloquial language where appropriate to the character. In the third person, these would be confined to dialogue.

First-person narration offers you the chance to make bold experiments in impersonation. You can pretend to be whatever you choose: judge, madwoman, vagrant, pop star, shopkeeper, wizard, ghost, anyone at all, even an animal or an object endowed with the power of thought. You may also, of course, use fictional versions of yourself in autobiographical stories, and this is often where new writers start.

. . . and limitations, with some possible remedies

There are certain hazards in the use of the first person. First-person stories can contain an over-concentration on the self with a tiresome repetition of 'I I' like telegraph poles stalking the landscape. This can be avoided by having the narrator describe other characters, the action or the setting.

89

It is necessary to have your narrator centre-stage, as he or she must be able to relate all the significant events of the story. Therefore, your narrator must be in a plausible position to know or discover the whole story.

It is an odd fact that first-person narrators who are like yourself may not always come across convincingly, especially if you are still close to the events you are describing. The novelist Deborah Moggach has observed that some of her least successful characters have been women of her own age and background, maybe because they are too close to her, 'too blurred to get into focus' (Moggach 1993: 133). If you experience this problem, it would be a good idea to try a third-person narration to give yourself some distance.

Author interview

Stevie Davies is a novelist who has notably used a wide range of viewpoints in her work. In a recent interview, I asked her about the challenges of first- person narration in relation to her novels *The Web of Belonging* (2004 [1997]) and *Kith and Kin* (2004).

In *The Web of Belonging*, the story is narrated by Jess, who is contentedly married to Jacob and happy to look after three of his elderly relatives in her own home. Her peaceable existence is shattered when Jacob abandons her without a word and Jess has to question the basis upon which she has lived so many years of her life.

Kith and Kin is narrated by Mara, who grew up in a close attachment to her cousin Frankie within the tight knot of an extended family in Swansea. When Mara sees a nostalgic film clip of Frankie in her youth, she is plunged into a confrontation with her past, forced to face unanswered questions about Frankie's life and death.

Here are some questions to think about as you read the extract from the interview:

- What are the challenges of first- person narration, according to Stevie Davies?
- How does she reveal to the reader what her first-person narrators do not know or understand?

Linda Anderson (LA): Do you find any problems with writing first-person narrators?

Stevie Davies (SD): Yes, first-person narration can be difficult. This is not generally recognised, I think. A beginning writer will be drawn to first person because obviously that is the closest to their own voice. But you need to escape from your own patterns, your habituated utterance. You need in any fiction which is not your own life history to adapt to your first person and to assimilate voices you may have heard or constellations of voices that you have heard and which you somehow or other, in some magical way, blend together to form your first person. When you've done that, I think it becomes quite hypnotic and you're there and you're with that assumed first person.

The other difficulty which goes with choosing first person is that it shuts you in. When I wrote *The Web of Belonging* I was intensely aware of being imprisoned in Jess's subjectivity. She herself is an imprisoned woman; she's saddled herself with dreadful burdens of caring for a large number of people and I found being within that consciousness extraordinarily claustrophobic. The way I found to break the stranglehold of her first-person subjectivity was to make the dialogue very powerful. If you just look at the book you can see that whole pages are given over to dialogue. I've been able to record the words and hence something of the mind processes of the people with whom she interacts, so as to give a kind of impression of the third-person world while using a first-person narrative point of view.

LA: In *Kith and Kin*, Mara says 'Versions are all you have' and that whole book is her excavation of the past, her coming to terms with the past and telling it to us. But with a first-person narration, there is always this difficulty of partiality. How do you counteract that?

SD: Mara is an honest rememberer and observer – but like all the rest of us she fakes the world to a certain degree – and the story is really Mara's recuperation of something like the reality of events that are long over and done with. She's a cold, brittle character who doesn't make relationships easily. She doesn't tell us why that is so although she's probably uneasily aware of it. But as the story progresses, we understand through the bruising events of the common childhood of Mara and Frankie why she came to be as she is.

Even in published fiction, we sometimes find stories in which all the characters sound the same. This happens when a writer can't break away from his or her own patterns of expression. To do so convincingly requires practice. Listen alertly to people speaking and note down interesting quirks or mannerisms. Using the actors' methods outlined in Chapter 3 will help you to assume voices different from your own.

Stevie Davies refers to two main strategies for overcoming the partial or unreliable vision of a first-person narration. You can include action and dialogue which contradicts or undermines the narrator's version. This contradiction can provide a shadowy counter-narrative, allowing us the satisfaction of understanding more than the narrator. The character-narrator is telling the story but is unaware of other possible interpretations which we may be picking up.

In cases where the narrator is a truth-seeker like Mara, it is the unfolding story itself, Mara's restored and better understood history, which enlarges both the character-narrator's perception and the reader's.

Activity 5.3   Writing

- Create a character who is different from you in one or two basic ways: body type, sex, age, wealth, intellect, or morality. Or you might like to use a character you have already been working on. Write up to 250 words from the first-person viewpoint of this character as he or she prepares to deal with a problem.
- Write this same character's account of a past situation. Give the voice authority and panache by avoiding any tone of hesitation or defeat. Finally, introduce another character who opposes your narrator's view of the story either subtly or dramatically. Use up to 500 words.

The narrator's voice

The reminiscent narrator

First-person narrators often look back, recounting stories from a distant past. Most of these narrators are endowed with astonishing memories, able to recall with exactitude every detail of conversations and events which may have happened decades ago.

Readers readily accept this convention and it is one that you may use. But it is also interesting to consider ways of acknowledging the unreliability of memory in such stories. Memory is fallible: we forget things or we make things up or believe what we were told. Our perspective shifts and we see our lives differently at different stages. We adapt our memories to support our current interpretations.

It can be powerful to admit uncertainty about all of the facts recalled. In Margaret Atwood's *The Blind Assassin* Iris Griffin, now in her eighties, relates the story of her and her sister's entwined lives. She often doubts her own recollections and admits that she has forgotten some supposedly memorable occasions. Here is part of her account of her wedding day:

> There was champagne, of course. There must have been: Winifred would not have omitted it. Others ate. Speeches were made, of which I remember nothing. Did we dance? I believe so. I didn't know how to dance, but I found myself on the dance floor, so some sort of stumbling-around must have occurred.
>
> (Atwood 2001 [2000]: 293)

Paradoxically, it is her struggle to remember and her partial retrievals of the past which inspire our trust.

Activity 5.4   Writing

Begin a story with the line:

> I thought I would always remember this, but over time it has become blurred.

Use a narrator who struggles to piece a memory together. The memory can be triggered by a chance meeting or the discovery of an old letter or photograph. Write up to 500 words.

The unreliable narrator

First-person narrators are inevitably fallible. You will have to decide how much your narrator can realistically know and understand. You must also choose whether they are truth-tellers or 'unreliable narrators', who can be either deliberate liars or self-deceivers.

The use of an unreliable narrator is a popular strategy in fiction. Bigots, madmen, innocents and liars address the reader directly. They can try to get us on their side or just assume values and views we don't share. Sometimes the unreliability is more subtle. Narrators may be ignorant of their own faults or motivations, usually in a way that causes disruption. Or they may be reliable in some ways but not in others. However florid or mild the unreliability, these kinds of stories force us to test the speaker's perspective against our own.

Given that we are inclined to trust first-person narratives, how do you signal unreliability? The author has to manipulate the narrator's tone to let us know that he or she is unreliable. The speaker says one thing but unwittingly reveals another. There may also be exaggerations, contradictions, obvious biases, or slips of the tongue.

For example, *The Yellow Wallpaper*, by Charlotte Perkins Gilman (1981 [1892]), shows a woman's mind derailing:

> Even when I go to ride, if I turn my head suddenly and surprise it –
> there is that smell!
>
> Such a peculiar odor too! I have spent hours in trying to analyze
> it, to find out what it smelled like.
>
> It is not bad – at first, and very gentle, but quite the subtlest,
> most enduring odor I ever met.
>
> In this damp weather it is awful, I wake up in the night and find
> it hanging over me.
>
> It used to disturb me at first. I thought seriously of burning the
> house – to reach the smell.
>
> (Gilman 1981 [1892]: 29)

The Remains of the Day, by Kazuo Ishiguro (1990 [1989]), gives a picture of complete self-deception in the story of Stevens, a butler who wrecks his life through a kind of snobbish servility to Lord Darlington, owner of a stately home. In this scene, we see Stevens prioritising his work duties over his father's dying.

> Indeed, my father's face had gone a dull reddish colour, like no
> colour I had seen on a living being. I heard Miss Kenton say
> softly behind me: 'His pulse is very weak.' I gazed at my father
> for a moment, touched his forehead slightly, then withdrew my
> hand.

'In my opinion,' Mrs Mortimer said, 'he's suffered a stroke.' With that, she began to cry. I noticed she reeked powerfully of fat and roast cooking. I turned away and said to Miss Kenton:

'This is most distressing. Nevertheless, I must now return downstairs.'

(Ishiguro 1990 [1989]: 104)

The whole sad tale of Stevens's abject deference to Lord Darlington, who turns out to be a Hitler appeaser and anti-Semite, and his driving away of Miss Kenton, who loves him, is told in a deadened and mirthless style. It would become tedious if it were not for our fascination with the gulf between that language and the reality of the events it attempts to describe.

Activity 5.5   Writing

- Write in the voice of a narrator who thinks of himself as deeply benevolent and generous. Show through his or her description of another person or group that he possesses a less charitable side. Use up to 150 words.
- Invent an unreliable narrator who is antagonistic towards a colleague. Again in up to 150 words, show that the narrator unknowingly envies or admires the other character.

Discussion

Here is an example of a colleague-loathing schoolteacher who is an unreliable narrator:

Thorpe is a pitiful specimen. Permanent shaving rash, whiny voice. He looks crumpled and pale as a parched mushroom. I used to have a fantasy about him living his eventless little life in the small cupboard under my stairs. Though I don't know how he managed to insinuate himself into my thoughts. I avoid the ordeal of trying to engage him in normal human conversation – it's hard enough with my pupils. Anyway, he would regard it a distraction from his seven-day working week. I suppose that's how he has collected all his promotions – by working constantly. No one seems to mind that his work is totally useless. I spotted at least twenty factual

95

errors in his latest proposal, some nonsense about cutting truancy figures. Not that I will say anything. One dreadful day very soon, this charmless creature will become my boss.

Lots of clues about unreliability here: the narrator claims to dislike and avoid Thorpe but appears almost obsessed with him. Her fantasy and her notion that he is responsible for her thinking about him hint at a possible denied attraction. Her determination to belittle his work and achievements seems to indicate envy.

Alternating first-person narrators

Novels are frequently composed of a number of first-person narrators, who each have their own chapters, sometimes headed by their names to avoid confusing the reader. It is another method for countering the inevitable partiality of a single narration.

For example, *The Beet Queen* by Louise Erdrich is a novel told through several first-person narrators, including the cousins Mary Adare and Sita Kozka. The story opens with Mary's account of being suddenly abandoned by her mother who runs off with a fairground pilot, The Great Omar, leaving behind her three children, including a baby boy. When the baby wakes, screaming with hunger, Mary is tricked into handing him over to a stranger who offers to get him fed and return him but he disappears. Mary and her brother Karl then stow away on an overnight train, heading for their aunt and uncle's home in Argus. On the way, Mary and Karl get separated and she ends up alone on her relatives' doorstep, clutching a trinket box.

Activity 5.6   Reading

Read the following extracts from *The Beet Queen*.
Make some brief notes about your response to Mary's account.
Then consider these questions as you read Sita's account:

- Does your view of the situation change?
- What about your feelings towards the characters – do they change?
- Why do you think the author chose this method of narration?

Mary Adare

I got up, put on one of Sita's hand-me-down pink dresses, and went out to the kitchen to wait for Uncle Pete. I cooked breakfast. That I made a good cup of coffee at age eleven and fried eggs was a source of wonder to my aunt and uncle, and an outrage to Sita. That's why I did it every morning until it became a habit to have me there.

I planned to be essential to them all, so depended upon that they could never send me off. I did this on purpose, because I soon found out that I had nothing else to offer. The day after I arrived in Argus and woke up to Sita's accusing questions, I had tried to give them what I thought was my treasure—the blue velvet box that held Mama's jewels. I did it in as grand a manner as I could, with Sita for a witness and with Pete and Fritzie sitting at the kitchen table. That morning, I walked in with my hair combed wet and laid the box between my uncle and aunt. I looked from Sita to Fritzie as I spoke.

'This should pay my way.'

[. . .]

'You don't have to pay us,' said Fritzie. 'Pete tell her. She doesn't have to pay us. Sit down, shut up, and eat.'

Fritzie spoke like that, joking and blunt. Pete was slower.

'Come. Sit down and forget about the money,' he said. 'You never know about your mother. ...' he added in an earnest voice that trailed away. Things had a way of evaporating under Fritzie's eyes, vanishing, getting sucked up into the blue heat of her stare. Even Sita had nothing to say.

'I want to give you this,' I said. 'I insist.'

'She insists,' exclaimed Aunt Fritzie. Her smile had a rakish flourish because one tooth was chipped in front. 'Don't insist,' she said.

But I would not sit down. I picked up a knife from the butter plate and started to pry the lock.

'Here now,' said Fritzie. 'Pete, help her.'

So Pete got up, fetched a screwdriver from the top of the icebox, sat down and jammed the end underneath the lock.

'Let her open it,' said Fritzie, when the lock popped up. Pete pushed the little round box across the table.

'I bet it's empty,' Sita said. She took a big chance saying that, but it paid off in spades and aces between us growing up because I lifted the lid a moment later and what she said was true. There was nothing of value in the box.

Stickpins. A few thick metal buttons off a coat. And a ticket describing a ring and the necklace set with garnets, pawned for practically nothing in Minneapolis.

There was silence. Even Fritzie was at a loss. Sita nearly buzzed off her chair in triumph but held her tongue until later, when she would crow. Pete put his hand on his head. I stood quietly, my mind working in a circle. If Sita had not been there I might have broken down and let the tears out again, like in the rooming house, but she kept me sharp.

(Erdrich 1987: 19–21)

Sita Kozka

My cousin Mary came in on the early freight train one morning, with nothing but an old blue keepsake box full of worthless pins and buttons. My father picked her up in his arms and carried her down the hallway into the kitchen. I was too old to be carried. He sat her down, then my mother said, 'Go clean the counters, Sita.' So I don't know what lies she told them after that.

Later on that morning, my parents put her to sleep in my bed.

When I objected to this, saying that she could sleep on the trundle, my mother said, 'Cry sakes, you can sleep there too, you know.' And that is how I ended up that night, crammed in the trundle, which is too short for me. I slept with my legs dangling out in the cold air. I didn't feel welcoming toward Mary the next morning, and who can blame me? Besides, on her first waking day in Argus, there were the clothes.

It is a good thing she opened the blue keepsake box at breakfast and found little bits of trash, like I said, because if I had not felt sorry for my cousin that day, I would not have stood for Mary and my mother ripping through my closet and bureau. 'This fits perfectly,' my mother said, holding up one of my favorite blouses, 'try it on!' And Mary did. Then she put it in her drawer, which was another thing. I had to clear out two of my bureau drawers for her.

'Mother,' I said, after this had gone on for some time and I was beginning to think I would have to wear the same three outfits all the next school year, 'Mother, this has really gone far enough.'

'Crap,' said my mother, who talks that way. 'Your cousin hasn't got a stitch.'

Yet she had half of mine by then, quite a wardrobe, and all the time it was increasing as my mother got more excited about dressing the poor orphan. But Mary wasn't really an orphan, although she played on that for sympathy. Her mother was still alive, even if she had left my cousin, which I doubted. I really thought that Mary just ran away from her mother because she could not appreciate Adelaide's style. It's not everyone who understands how to use their good looks to the best advantage. My Aunt Adelaide did. She was always my favorite, and I just died for her to visit. But she didn't come often because my mother couldn't understand style either.

(Erdrich 1987: 27–28)

Discussion

Mary's story could hardly be more involving or heart-rending. Dumped cruelly and without warning by her mother, suddenly responsible for herself and her brothers, and penniless, she shows great resourcefulness and courage. But she gets parted from both of her brothers and ends up on her relatives' doorstep utterly alone and bereft. She has reached a place of safety but with a resident enemy, Sita, the expert tormentor. The scene in which Mary presents the trinket box to her aunt and uncle, declaring that the contents will pay her way, ratchets up the anguish. As the box is wrenched open to reveal its worthless trinkets and pawnshop ticket, we witness the final stripping of Mary's pride and faith. The girl's mortification is complete and so is our sympathy . . .

But then we read Sita's account of Mary's sudden arrival and her own sense of being ousted. We start to see that she is a child too, and suddenly not an only child any longer but someone propelled into a kind of sibling relationship without the usual years of learning how to share. We learn too that she sees Mary's mother, her aunt Adelaide, as a glamorous misunderstood figure, someone she identifies with. She does not believe Mary's accusations against her. Without losing sight of Mary's suffering, we can begin to see that Sita's spitefulness and resentment are understandable.

The author is likely to have chosen this method of alternating narrations precisely because of its jolting effect. It can cause us to switch our allegiance from one character to another, or at least to see things in a more complex way without the comfort of being able to label characters as 'goodies' and 'baddies'. The 'truth' is difficult to locate and cannot be fully delivered by one character's perspective. The presentation of more than one version of events honours this fact and also gives the reader the chance to work things out for themselves.

It is a demanding method, though, and one that is more appropriate for the novel than the short story, which has less room for multiple voices. The writer has to create a different voice for each narrator and try to make them equally interesting, otherwise the reader's attention will flag when their favourite speaker is 'offstage'.

Activity 5.7 Writing

Invent two characters who are in dispute, for example colleagues competing for a promotion, a father and daughter quarrelling over her choice of husband, divorced parents arguing about their child's education. Or choose your own scenario. Write alternating first-person accounts of the conflict. Try to make each version persuasive and sympathetic. They should both seem plausible, thereby complicating the issue. Use up to 250 words for each account.

Form of narration

First-person stories may be told in a variety of ways, chiefly through:

- *interior monologue* – the private self-communions of the character, which may be verbalised thoughts and reflections or, occasionally, diary writings;
- *dramatic monologue* – in which the character addresses another person or a particular audience in speech or sometimes by letter;
- *detached autobiography* – in which the narrator tells about his or her past life, the passage of time enabling him or her to achieve a fairly dispassionate stance.

The first two modes place the reader in the position of eavesdropper; the latter puts us in the position of acknowledged audience.

The Beet Queen is an example of detached autobiography addressed to a general reader in a highly self-conscious and constructed way. Diary writing and letters are worth experimenting with in stories where a more casual and intimate mode of revelation is appropriate.

The Bridget Jones diaries are the most famous recent examples of 'private' journals. Notice the shorthand style in the opening of *Bridget Jones: The edge of reason*:

Monday 27 January

9st 3 (total fat groove), boyfriends 1 (hurrah!), shags 3 (hurrah!), calories 2,100, calories used up by shags 600, so total calories 1,500 (exemplary).

7.15 a.m. Hurrah! The wilderness years are over. For four weeks and five days now have been in functional relationship with adult male thereby proving am not love pariah as previously feared. Feel marvellous, rather like Jemima Goldsmith or similar radiant newlywed opening cancer hospital in veil while everyone imagines her in bed with Imran Khan.

(Fielding 2000 [1999]: 3)

Activity 5.9   Reading

Read the following extract from the opening pages of J.M. Coetzee's *Age of Iron*. This is an example of a first-person narration addressed to another character. In Cape Town, Elizabeth Curren has just learned that she has cancer.

- To whom is the story told?
- What effect does this have?

With what slow steps did I enter this empty house, from which every echo has faded, where the very tread of footsole on board is flat and dull! How I longed for you to be here, to hold me, comfort me! I begin to understand the true meaning of the embrace. We embrace to be embraced. We embrace our children to be folded in the arms of the future, to pass ourselves on beyond death, to be transported. That is how it was when I embraced you, always. We bear children in order to be mothered by them. Home truths, a mother's truth: from now to the end that is all you will hear from me. So: how I longed for you! How I longed to be able to go upstairs to you, to sit on your bed, run my fingers through your hair, whisper in your ear as I did on school mornings, 'Time to get up!' And then, when you turned over, your body blood-warm, your breath milky, to take you in my arms in what we called 'giving Mommy a big hug,' the secret meaning of which, the meaning never spoken, was that Mommy should not be sad, for she would not die but live on in you.

To live! You are my life; I love you as I love life itself. In the mornings I come out of the house and wet my finger and hold it up to the wind. When the chill is from the north-west, from your quarter, I stand a long time sniffing, concentrating my attention in the hope that across ten thousand miles of land and sea some breath will reach me of the milkiness you still carry with you behind your ears, in the fold of your neck.

The first task laid on me, from today: to resist the craving to share my death. Loving you, loving life, to forgive the living and take my leave without bitterness. To embrace death as my own, mine alone.

To whom this writing then? The answer: to you but not to you; to me; to you in me.

(Coetzee 1991: 4–5)

Discussion

The narrator's story is in the form of a letter to her daughter. It also comes across partly as a private piece of writing, an unburdening prompted by sudden bad news.The effect is poignant and convincing. It seems more plausible that a woman told she will die soon would want to tell her dearest relative rather than some phantom general reader. The fact that her daughter is in America adds to the bleakness of the narrator's isolation.

Choosing a form

You will need to decide your approach at the outset. To whom is the story addressed? To the character-narrator's self, to another character, to a general reader? In what form? How much time has elapsed between the events of the story and its telling? There are stories told as the events are happening, stories told shortly afterwards, and stories recorded long afterwards. If your narrator is remembering events from long ago, how much has he or she changed? Is he still emotionally involved? What is her attitude to her younger self? Given that the narrator already knows the entire story, to what extent is he inclined to control the pace of revelations? For example, in *The Beet Queen*, Mary lets us know in the opening pages that she stayed at her aunt and uncle's house permanently: 'This was where I would sleep every night for the rest of my life' (Erdrich 1987:18). Therefore there is no 'suspense' about the outcome; the fascination will come from seeing how the relationships worked out.

Conclusion

First-person narrative requires the creation of a compelling, single voice telling its own story in a way that produces a strong sense of realism. Of course, there is a great deal of artfulness and artifice in the production of this 'realism'. Such stories use the models of personal confession, the diary, autobiography, or memoir. Both first-person fictions and 'life writing' have enjoyed immense popularity in recent years and the boundary between them has blurred. For example, Andrea Ashworth's *Once in a House on Fire* (1998) is an autobiography which reads like a novel; Margaret Atwood's *Cat's Eye* (1990) is a novel which reads like an autobiography.

References

Ashworth, Andrea (1998) *Once in a House on Fire*, London: Picador.
Atwood, Margaret (1990) *Cat's Eye*, London: Virago Press.
Atwood, Margaret (2001 [2000]) *The Blind Assassin*, London: Virago.
Coetzee, J.M. (1991) *Age of Iron*, London: Penguin.
Davies, Stevie (2004 [1997]) *The Web of Belonging*, London: Phoenix.
Davies, Stevie (2004) *Kith and Kin*, London: Weidenfeld & Nicolson.
Erdrich, Louise (1987) *The Beet Queen*, London: Pavanne/Pan Books.
Fielding, Helen (2000 [1999]) *Bridget Jones: The edge of reason*, London: Picador.
Gilman, Charlotte Perkins (1981 [1892]) *The Yellow Wallpaper*, London: Virago.

Hind, Angela (producer) (2005) interview, A215 Creative Writing CDI, 'Writing Fiction', Milton Keynes: The Open University/Pier Productions.

Hodgins, Jack (1994 [1993]) *A Passion for Narrative: A guide for writing fiction*, New York: St. Martin's Press.

Ishiguro, Kazuo (1990 [1989]) *The Remains of the Day*, London: Faber & Faber.

McCabe, Patrick (1993 [1992]) *The Butcher Boy*, London: Picador.

Moggach, Deborah (1993) 'Fleshing my characters' in Clare Boylan (ed.) *The Agony and the Ego: The art and strategy of fiction writing explored*, London: Penguin.

Roth, Philip (2001 [2000]) *The Human Stain*, London: Vintage.

6

Point of view: degrees of knowing

Linda Anderson

Third-person narration

In a third-person point of view, the writer uses 'he', 'she', or 'they' rather than the first-person 'I'. There are three possible strategies to choose from:

- *Limited omniscience* – where the narrator knows everything that a particular character may see, feel and know but knows nothing more about other protagonists than the character-narrator.
- *Omniscience* – where the narrator knows everything about the events, places and all of the characters, even things which the characters themselves may be incapable of knowing.
- *Objective point of view* – where the narrator knows only what he or she can observe externally, as in a 'fly-on-the-wall' documentary, and recounts this neutrally.

Limited omniscience

This technique is the most commonly used because it enables the writer to capture in the fullest way both the inside and outside views of a character. It is also known as 'single character point of view' because the author allows us to see the world through the perspective of the chosen character. It combines the intimacy of the first-person point of view with a degree of distance as the hidden narrator is able to paraphrase the thoughts of the character, as well as to organise and comment on the story.

Here is an example from a novel-in-progress, *The Tree House*, by Amanda Hodgkinson. The story is about a Polish family who come to live in England after suffering terrible ordeals during the Second World War. The man, Janusz, tries to become an accepted member of his local community but his attempts are undermined by his wife and son. They have survived by hiding and living wild in the birch forests of the Polish countryside and cannot adapt to their new life.

> Gilbert grips the top of the wooden fence. He lowers his voice and Janusz steps closer. 'I've got a bottle of scotch in the garden shed. Come over when the women are out shopping on Saturday morning. We can talk about the war.'
>
> Janusz does not want to remember the war. Always go forwards, he says. You can't live in the past. What's the point of remembering things? It's all gone. The past is past. 'That would be nice,' he says, handing Gilbert back his matches.
>
> (Hodgkinson n.d.)

An anonymous narrator reports everything from Janusz's perspective. It is as if the narrator and reader are confidants. The narrator's ability to convey the main character's inner thoughts, as well as to observe his behaviour from the outside, shows us the tension between Janusz's unexpressed and expressed feelings. In just a few lines, we get a poignant sense of the outsider's dilemma, how much he suppresses in order to fit in.

In first-person narration, we get direct access to the character's consciousness. In third-person limited narration, there is still intimate access to the character's consciousness through the method of 'free indirect style', a fusion of third- and first-person perspectives first developed at the end of the eighteenth century.

In the following example from Virginia Woolf's story, *Lappin and Lapinova*, Rosalind is a few days into her honeymoon. Notice the double vision at work. We get elegant reportage from an invisible narrator mixed with observations using the character's own sense impressions and chatty phrases.

Ernest was a difficult name to get used to. It was not the name she would have chosen. She would have preferred Timothy, Antony, or Peter. He did not look like Ernest either. [. . .] But here he was. Thank goodness he did not look like Ernest – no. But what did he look like? She glanced at him sideways. Well, when he was eating toast he looked like a rabbit. Not that anyone else would have seen a likeness to a creature so diminutive and timid in this spruce, muscular young man with the straight nose, the blue eyes, and the very firm mouth. But that made it all the more amusing. His nose twitched very slightly when he ate. So did her pet rabbit's.

(Woolf 1949, quoted in Lee 1987: 20)

Activity 6.1   Writing

- Recall an argument you have had with someone. Write about the quarrel from your opponent's point of view, using third-person limited omniscience. The objective here is to practise empathy with points of view that antagonise you in reality. Empathy is not always easy to attain but it expands the fiction writer's imaginative range like nothing else. Write up to 300 words.
- Take one of your own memories and cast it in a third-person limited point of view. Don't aim to write it as a strictly 'truthful' account. Release it into a fictional story, feeling free to invent different details, deepen the drama or change the outcome. The aim is to give you practice in distancing yourself from your own experiences and using them as a fund of fictional material. Write up to 500 words.

Omniscient narrator

The third-person omniscient voice is the most wide-ranging and authoritative point of view. An omniscient narrator can enter the consciousness of any character; describe that character's appearance, speech, behaviour, thoughts, history, and motivations; know what has happened elsewhere or in the past and what will happen in the future; intervene in the narrative to make asides, such as comments on the action, forewarnings of future events, or wise reflections on life.

Notice the authoritative tone and summarising style of this extract from Anton Chekhov's *Lady with Lapdog*.

He was not yet forty, but he had a twelve-year-old daughter and two schoolboy sons. He had been married off when he was still in his second year at the university, and his wife seemed to him now to be almost twice his age. She was a tall, black-browed woman, erect, dignified, austere, and, as she liked to describe herself, a 'thinking person'. She was a great reader, preferred the new 'advanced' spelling, called her husband by the more formal 'Dimitry' and not the familiar 'Dmitry'; and though he secretly considered her not particularly intelligent, narrow-minded, and inelegant, he was afraid of her and disliked being at home.

(Chekhov 1964 [1899]: 264)

Third-person omniscience was a popular choice in nineteenth-century novels where the author might even address the audience as 'dear reader' or 'gentle reader'. It became unfashionable as discoveries in psychology and science throughout the twentieth century eroded belief in the possibility of absolute 'truth' and impartiality. A.S. Byatt wrote recently about the prevalence of first-person narratives in modern historical novels and felt obliged to speak up for her own preference for 'the unfashionable Victorian third-person narrator' (Byatt 2001, quoted in Lodge 2003 [2002]: 86)

But omniscience remains a standard method for certain 'genre' narratives, like science fiction, and it also appears to be making a comeback in literary fiction. For example, later in this chapter you will read the opening of Rick Moody's *Purple America*, a novel from the point of view of an omniscient narrator with a passionate, erudite voice and a lot to say about the treatment of the elderly and about the dangers of the nuclear power industry. Omniscience could be right for you or for certain stories you want to tell if you have a distinctive style or a lot to say about your characters, theme, or period of time.

Shifting third-person method

A lot of contemporary writers use omniscience in a modified form with minimal authorial intrusions. They use alternating third-person subjective viewpoints.

108

For a contemporary example, here is an extract from Pat Barker's *Another World*, a novel with multiple points of view. Think about these questions as you read:

- What is the impact of the shift from the mother's mind to the teenage son's?
- How much authorial intrusion is there?

Jasper, who hates the hot plastic car seat, stiffens his legs till they're like planks. Fran, holding a heavy toddler at arm's length, back aching, stomach getting in the way of everything, pendulous breasts each with a swamp of sweat underneath, thinks, This is stupid. She stops, lets Jasper get out, and plays with him for a while, pretendy chases and tickling and incey-wincey-spider-climbed-up-the-spout, then when he's curled up and helpless with giggles she slips him quickly into the seat and clicks the buckle. He opens his mouth to scream, but she crashes the gears, turns the radio on full blast, starts to sing 'Incey Wincey Spider' at the top of her voice, until Jasper, bowling along the open road, breath snatched out of his mouth, deafened by the noise, forgets what he's crying about, and points at the shadows of leaves flickering across the roof. ''Ook, 'ook.'

'Yeah,' says Gareth sourly. ''Ook.'

Fran slips one hand into her blouse and surreptitiously rubs the sweat, flaps the cotton, does what she can to dry off. When she was a girl – back in the middle Jurassic – she'd been one of the last in her class to hold a pencil under them. Get pencil cases in there now. Be a pencil factory soon if she doesn't do something about this bloody saggy bra. 'Look, Gareth,' she says, trying to keep the lines of communication open. 'There's your new school.'

And why the fuck would anybody want to look at that? Gareth thinks.

But look at it he does. It's empty now, of course, in the middle of August, a long, low huddle of buildings, one of them with its windows boarded up, because last winter the pipes burst and flooded the labs and there's no money to get them repaired. Though Digger says it wasn't burst pipes, it was his brother Paul and a gang of lads broke in and left the taps running. Gareth doesn't know whether to believe him or not.

(Barker 1999: 131–2)

Discussion

Fran's point of view is so involving and intimate, even making us privy to her bodily discomfort, that the sudden shift into Gareth's coarse, angry thought is dramatic. It is the sort of switch that could annoy or confuse a reader but Barker has established her method in this novel from the start. It is written as a series of limited omniscient voices alternating within the same chapters and linked by occasional authorial commentary, as here, giving us information about the school: 'But look at it he does. It's empty now, of course, in the middle of August, a long, low huddle of buildings, one of them with its windows boarded up, because last winter the pipes burst and flooded the labs and there's no money to get them repaired.'

If you want to tell a story using multiple characters' viewpoints without much direct intervention from an omniscient narrator, establish your method early on to accustom the reader. Signal each shift into another point of view by creating a slightly different tone and voice. It is also reader-friendly to use separate chapters or sections for each viewpoint, signalling changes by starting a new paragraph.

Objective point of view

The third-person objective point of view is impersonal. The writer is restricted to recording what may be witnessed from external appearances and facts. He or she will not enter the characters' heads or offer any interpretations or judgements. The technique is similar to that of film in that everything must be inferred from gestures, expressions, actions, dialogue, and silences. This technique can have a lot of appeal for writers and readers who enjoy a pared down, austere style. The reader has to ponder signs and clues in order to figure things out.

Ernest Hemingway is the acknowledged master of this technique and it is worth reading his novels or stories to get a sense of how he does it. His style is remarkably spare and this is the result of ruthless revision and editing: he went through thirty-six possible endings for *A Farewell to Arms*; he deleted the first fifteen pages of *The Sun Also Rises*. He often allows characters' body language to speak for itself – to convey a sense of rage or sorrow too raw for words. Silences and missing information haunt his stories. His theory was that 'you could omit anything if you knew that you omitted it and the omitted part would strengthen the story and make people feel more than they understood' (Lodge 2003 [2002]: 70).

Activity 6.3   Reading

Here is an example of third-person objective narration using the Middleton family scenario we began with in Chapter 5. Let's suppose that the wayward son, Simon, has been caught drug-dealing at school and has been sent home pending a police investigation. He has locked himself in his room, refusing to speak. The mother, Susannah, is alone until her daughter, Amy, returns from school.

- As you read, consider whether you can tell what the characters are thinking or feeling?

Susannah Middleton gripped her little Jack Russell terrier with both hands but he squirmed free and pranced around the room, leaping on and off the chairs and sofa.

'Good boy, good boy, come here,' Susannah coaxed the dog, who barked back at her. 'Go away then,' she shouted. A cup of tea sat on the nest of tables by her side. She lifted the drink, rejected it at once and strode over to the drinks cabinet, which she tried to open. 'Oh, the key, where did I put the damn key?'

At that moment, there was the sound of the front door unlocking. Susannah outstretched her arms just as Amy burst into the room. 'Oh, thank god you're home. . .'

Amy bent down to grab the dog, scooping him up into a bundle with her satchel and mobile phone. Her mother wrapped her arms around herself.

'Why is Zak in here, mum?' The dog started to whimper and yelp as if joining a campaign to get himself excluded. 'He's going mental. He knows he's not allowed in here, don't you, you little monster.'

Susannah turned away to face the window. 'I just wanted some comfort. He won't even let me stroke him.'

'What's wrong?'

'Your brother's upstairs.'

Amy laughed. 'It's only me who's supposed to hate him being around.'

Susannah looked straight at her, 'He's been suspended from school. I had to go and fetch him. As if he's some . . . plague-carrier!'

'What's he done?'

'What has he allegedly done, you mean?'

Amy waited in silence.

'They've accused him of taking drugs . . . and selling them. They've informed the police.'

Amy sat down, keeping the dog on her lap. 'Why is he upstairs?'

'Look at how quiet Zak is with you! Is he afraid of me or something?'

'What did you say to Simon, mum?'

'I begged him to tell me what really happened. If someone planted the drugs on him, or if he's been bullied into taking the blame. I told him that I believe in him, we all do. No son of mine would get involved in drugs.'

'Are you going to disown him, then?'

'No, of course not. I would never disown him, no matter what he did.'

'So you admit that he might have done something?'

'You're so disloyal. He's your brother!'

Amy cleared her throat and stood up. 'I could stay home if you want. I'll cancel my violin lesson.'

Susannah started pacing up and down. 'But you've only got four lessons booked this whole term.'

'Mum, I've been playing violin since I was nine!'

Neither spoke for a few moments. Susannah stopped in front of the mirror. She patted her hair and wiped her eyes.

'No son of mine would dabble in drugs,' she said sternly, stressing each syllable.

'That's right. He doesn't dabble. He's in it up to his neck.'

'What would you know?'

'He used to say you even had eyes in the back of your head. But what use is that if your head is buried in the sand?'

Amy marched to the door.

'Where are you going?'

'Upstairs to see Simon.'

Susannah moved to follow. Amy wagged her finger: 'You stay here.'

'Who, Zak?' Susannah whispered.

'Him as well.'

Discussion

Everything is indicated through physical gestures, actions, and the way the characters speak as well as their actual words. We see that the normally super-controlled Susannah is agitated and desperate. She seeks comfort and is thwarted at every turn – both the dog and the daughter avoid her embrace; the drinks cupboard is locked. When Amy stoops to lift the dog, ignoring her mother's outstretched arms, Susannah caresses herself, for self-comfort or perhaps to mask the rejection. When she admits to vulnerable feelings: 'I just wanted some comfort', she turns away from her daughter. This could be a way of showing hopelessness about getting any sympathy. But she looks straight at Amy when she tells her the news. All of her protestations show a determined but shaky denial. Her most poignant speech is when she deflects Amy's question about why Simon is upstairs. 'Look at how quiet Zak is with you. Is he afraid of me or something?' It's easy to see this as a leakage of her shadowy realisation that it is her *son* who fears her. When she repeats her declaration that 'No son of mine would dabble in drugs', she looks at her own reflection in the mirror. It is as if she is affirming an image of herself that is under threat.

Despite the mother's adamant talk, it is Amy who is in charge in this scene. Her initial questions are terse and to the point. 'What's wrong?' and 'What's he done?' But she focuses on what the mother has done: 'What did you say to Simon?' This suggests that she understands why Simon has fled to his room. She tries to move her mother out of her brittle defences by exposing the terrible logic of her stance: if her son could not possibly be a wrongdoer, will Simon cease to be her son? When Susannah accuses her of disloyalty, Amy clears her throat, her first sign of nervousness, and offers to stay home. This is like an oblique disavowal of a lack of loyalty. Exasperated finally by her mother's refusal to face the situation, Amy's words become hard-hitting and her actions decisive – marching towards the door, wagging her finger. By contrast, Susannah is now reduced to whispering.

113

We can divine a lot about the relationship between the mother and daughter from this scene. The way that Amy avoids her mother's embrace indicates that demonstrations of affection are rare. We get a glimpse of the depth of estrangement of this woman from both of her teenage children.

Your own speculations about the underlying emotions of the characters may be different from mine. Each reader fills in the gaps for themselves. This degree of reader-involvement in interpreting stories is one of the assets of the objective point of view.

Consistency of point of view

Once you have chosen a point of view for a particular story, it is important to stick to it with clarity and consistency. But this is a skill which requires practice. Try out the different points of view to find your own strengths. Each time you read a new novel, take a look at the point(s) of view chosen by the author. Make notes in your writer's notebook about how effective you think they are.

Point of view errors tend to occur with the use of third-person omniscience. Unlimited powers can be hard to handle! Because an omniscient author may enter the mind of any character, new writers sometimes dutifully report what is going on in everyone's mind, flitting back and forth from head to head. Here's an invented example:

> The restaurant seemed suddenly too noisy and hot. Robert wished they could be somewhere else, but he had promised Anthea this big celebration. She was secretly bristling with anger at his choice of venue as she ordered the most boring dishes on the menu. Their waitress hovered reluctantly, worrying about the ladder in her tights. It had already been a long shift.

A reader is likely to get baffled and annoyed by this sort of writing. It is impossible to tell who is an important character and who is secondary. Do we need to invest a lot of attention in the waitress or will she disappear soon from the narrative? The flitting from head to head is dizzying, like those films shot with a hand-held camera veering from one speaker to the next.

The way to make this example consistent is to lock in to one observing mind. Let's make Robert the viewpoint character here. We can indicate the same facts as he sees them or interprets them.

The restaurant seemed suddenly too noisy and hot. Robert wished they could be somewhere else, but he had promised Anthea this big celebration. She didn't exactly look grateful, though, and was ordering dishes he knew she disliked. The sullen waitress wasn't helping to dispel his anxieties.

Sometimes a point of view shift happens in mid-sentence:

She dreaded her teacher's response and braced herself for a stony-faced critique but he was impressed, even starting to wonder if she might be a star student.

This kind of shift is disturbing. Again, it works better if we lock in to the original observer and show the teacher's response through her viewpoint.

She dreaded her teacher's response and braced herself for a stony-faced critique but he was clearly impressed, even saying that her essay was one of the best he had ever seen.

In the following example, we start off in a single character point of view but then in mid-sentence shift into an external view of him. As he cannot know how his own face changes or what effect it has, this is a jarring breach of the point of view.

He liked the look of his new tenant. A trainee solicitor! She would add a bit of class to the place. He caught the drift of her scent and smiled at her, transforming his pinched face into unexpected charm.

These kinds of slippages and muddles happen easily, even to experienced writers, especially in the creation of first drafts when you are trying to include as many significant details as possible. So don't worry about them but do look out for them. Mid-sentence shifts are particularly ugly and destabilising and should be avoided.

Multiple points of view and flitting from head to head *may* be used but must be handled cautiously. It is usually best to confine your viewpoint characters to a few and not to move around within the same page. But as with most general principles, this is not a 'rule'. You might decide that the power to move briefly into different minds suits a particular story you want to tell. For example, Tim Lott's 2003 novel *Rumours of a Hurricane* opens with a drunk, suicidal man stumbling into the path of a lorry. The narration takes us into the thoughts of bystanders at the scene of the accident, then ambulance men and a surgeon, none of whom will appear again in the novel.

> The journey to the hospital is uneventful. In the wake of the ambulance, a few of the abandoned pedestrians are still staring at the brown penumbra of blood, are still guiltily enjoying the excitement. The paramedics are thinking about how long is left on their shift. The man on the stretcher is delirious. His thoughts are like scattered, broken glass, each containing a reflection connected, yet unconnectable, with a larger picture. He thinks of a wide boulevard dotted with yew trees. [. . .]
>
> At the hospital doctors and nurses crowd around him as he is unloaded. Something in him is grateful for the attention, even flattered by it. He thought he had forgone such privileges long ago. Injury is elevating. People grant you respect.
>
> Soon after the unloading, the man loses consciousness. He has been given a general anaesthetic. The surgeon, a cynical, hunched-over sexagenarian with a hatred of life that has somehow been generated by its endless sluicing through his hands, can hardly find the wherewithal to operate. He has taken his saviour's knife to too many street roughs and drunks and hopeless cases with their ruined insides, keeping him from spending valuable time on those he thinks of as more valuable people, those he believes misfortune, rather than personal weakness, has laid low. He hates what he tries to save; a futile drain on resources.
>
> (Lott 2003: 9)

The story is about the contrasting fortunes of Charlie and Maureen Buck and the way they both change during the get-rich-quick eighties – the woman liberating herself, the man losing everything. Most of the novel focuses on these two characters, but because it is partly a 'state-of-nation' picture, a study of the impact of Thatcherism on culture and morality, the author establishes this wider significance at the outset with his snapshots of bystanders and medical workers. The effect of the opening is also to distance us from Charlie Buck, the ruined and desolate accident victim. The rest of the story will bring us into a close knowledge of him and make us care about his disasters. So there is a strong purpose in the free-floating omniscience at the start of the novel.

The point is that you may do whatever you decide so long as you know what you're doing and stay in control.

Activity 6.4   Writing

Imagine a conflict between two characters. An elderly man meets his estranged son. A woman decides to call off her wedding. A parent confronts a teacher about school bullying. Or invent your own scenario.

Write about the situation three times from three different points of view, using up to 300 words for each version:

- third-person limited omniscient;
- third-person omniscient;
- third-person objective.

Discussion

This exercise can help you to identify your own strengths and preferences. Did you enjoy presenting the workings of your main character's mind? Or did you prefer to keep the reader at a greater distance? Which version works best for your story and why? You might like to expand your favourite version into a completed story.

Some unusual points of view

First- and third-person points of view are the most commonly used. Once you have become familiar with them, it can be refreshing to try out more unusual strategies.

Second-person narration

In a second-person narration, the main character is referred to as 'you', which almost assigns the reader a role as player in the unfolding story. It is a provocative device, which can meet with resistance from the reader. 'You are standing watching the sunset . . .' (*No, I'm not.*) . . . 'when the door is flung open' (*No, it's not.*) . . . 'and Sam is pointing a gun at your head' . . . (*Wrong again!*) But when the method succeeds, it can involve the reader deeply in the story.

117

Activity 6.5 Reading

Read the following two extracts. The first is from John McGahern's *The Dark*, which is about a troubled adolescent boy. The second is Jamaica Kincaid's *Girl*.

- What different kinds of impact are achieved by the use of second-person narration in these pieces?

Extract 1

After a quarrel with his father, the narrator contemplates his father's boots and is overcome with compassion.

He went muttering and complaining that way to bed. And then, when he was gone, the wave of remorse that came. You'd troubled him, and for what? Did it matter what was prayed for? If it gave him satisfaction to pray for success why not let him, it would make no difference except he'd not be upset as now. Stupid vanity had caused it all. The house had gone to bed. You were alone in the kitchen. You wanted to say to him you were sorry but you weren't able.

His boots, wet from the grass, stood drying by the raked fire. They started to take on horrible fascination.

They were your father's boots, close to the raked fire. They'd been put there to dry for morning. Their toes touched where the ashes spilled out from the fire on the concrete, boots wet from the grass. Your father's feet had been laced in their black leather, leather over walking flesh. They'd walk in his hopes, be carried over the ground, till they grew worn, past mending, and were discarded for the new pair from Curley's, on and on, over the habitual fields, lightly to the football matches in Reegan's field on Sundays, till the feet themselves wore, boots taken off his dying feet. Corns of the flesh against the leather. All the absurd anxiety and delight and heedlessness the boots carried. They stood so utterly quiet by the fire, the feet that they'd cover resting between sheets to wear them through another day. The boots were so calm there. They would not move. You touched them in fascination, they did not stir, only the rough touch of wet boot leather against the fingertips. One lace was broken, replaced by white twine.

How could you possibly hurt or disturb anyone? Hadn't the feet that wore the boots, all that life moving in boot leather, enough to contend with, from morning to night to death, without you heaping on more burden, from sheer egotism. Did it matter to the boots, moving or still, whether your success was prayed for or not? Why couldn't you allow people to do the small things that pleased them? In this same mood you did what you had never done and went and knocked on his door.

'Who's that? What do you want?'

'I'm sorry over the prayers.'

'It's a bit late in the day to be sorry now, easy to be sorry when the harm's done, such heathen rubbish, easy to know why you're sorry. It's more than sorry you ought to be——'

Anger rose as the voice continued to complain out of the darkness of the bedroom. The same boots could kick and trample. You couldn't stand it, you'd only meant well, that was all.

'Forget it for God's sake. I just said I was sorry,' you said and closed the door sharply to go troubled and angry through the kitchen to your own bedroom.

(McGahern 1983: 130–2)

Extract 2

Wash the white clothes on Monday and put them on the stone heap; wash the colour clothes on Tuesday and put them on the clothes-line to dry; don't walk barehead in the hot sun; cook pumpkin fritters in very hot sweet oil; soak your little cloths right after you take them off; when buying cotton to make yourself a nice blouse, be sure that it doesn't have gum on it, because that way it won't hold up well after a wash; soak salt fish overnight before you cook it; is it true that you sing benna in Sunday school?; always eat your food in such a way that it won't turn someone else's stomach; on Sundays try to walk like a lady and not like the slut you are so bent on becoming; don't sing benna in Sunday school; you mustn't speak to wharf-rat boys, not even to give directions; don't eat fruits on the street—flies will follow you; *but I don't sing benna on Sundays at all and never in Sunday school*; this is how to sew on a button; this is how to make a button-hole for the button you have just sewed on; this is how to hem a dress when you see the hem coming down and so to prevent yourself from looking like the slut I know you are so bent on becoming; this is how you iron your father's khaki shirt so that it doesn't have a crease; this is how you iron your father's khaki pants so that they don't have a crease; this is how you grow okra—far from the house, because okra tree harbors red ants; when you are growing dasheen, make sure it gets plenty of water or else it makes your throat itch when you are eating it; this is how you sweep a corner; this is how you sweep a whole house; this is how you sweep a yard; this is how you smile to someone you don't like too much; this is how you smile to someone you don't like at all; this is how you smile to someone you like completely; this is how you set a table for tea; this is how you set a table for dinner; this is how you set a table for dinner with an important guest; this is how you set a table for lunch; this is how you set a table for breakfast; this is how to behave in the presence of men who don't know you very well, and this way they won't recognize immediately the slut I have warned you against becoming; be sure to wash every day, even if it is with your own spit; don't squat down to play marbles—you are not a boy, you know; don't pick people's flowers—you might catch something; don't throw stones at blackbirds, because it might not be a black-bird at all; this is how to make a bread pudding; this is how to make doukona; this is how to make pepper pot; this is how to make a good medicine for a cold; this is how to make a good medicine to throw away a child before it even becomes a child; this is how to catch a fish; this is how to throw back a fish you don't like, and that way something bad won't fall on you; this is how to bully a man; this is how a man bullies you; this is how to love a man, and if this doesn't work there are other ways, and if they don't work don't feel too bad about giving up; this is how to spit up in the air if you feel like it, and this is how to move quick so that it doesn't fall on you; this is how to make ends meet; always squeeze bread to make sure it's fresh; *but what if the baker won't let me feel the bread?*; you mean to say that after all you are really going to be the kind of woman who the baker won't let near the bread?

(Kincaid 1983: 3–5)

Second-person narration in *The Dark* creates a claustophobic mood of loneliness and self-questioning. The 'you' seems to refer to a divided self, as if the character is so wounded or alienated that he has had to become his own confidant.

This method is best used for stories where the writer wants to convey the universality of an individual situation or for stories about lonely, obsessive characters. It is difficult to sustain over a long narrative as it can become airless and tedious, so most writers alternate it with other points of view in long narratives.

Jamaica Kincaid's *Girl* shows an inventive use of the second person. The girl's mind is saturated with a barrage of internalised orders from a controlling mother-figure. Without resorting to obvious 'message', the piece seems to make a statement about female conditioning.

Activity 6.6   Writing

Now try this method out for yourself.

- Invent a lonely character in some kind of confinement, for example a prisoner on remand, an infatuated person whose love is unrequited, or a homesick student at boarding school. Using the second person, describe a good memory from the character's past and compare it with their present predicament. Write up to 500 words.
- Using *Girl* as a model, write a set of intimidating or satirical instructions in the second person about how to be a writer. Write 150 to 200 words.

Stream of consciousness

'Stream of consciousness' was the phrase first used by the psychologist William James to describe the ceaseless, random flow of thoughts, ideas, memories, and fantasies in people's minds. Dorothy Richardson, James Joyce, and Virginia Woolf were ground-breaking practitioners of stream-of-consciousness in fiction. These writers tried to mimic psychological reality, capturing the crazy paving of the human mind.

Here is a brief extract from Molly Bloom's famous 63-page, 1-sentence interior monologue which concludes Joyce's *Ulysses*.

> [. . .] what could you make of a man like that I'd rather die 20 times over than marry another of their sex of course hed never find another woman like me to put up with him the way I do know me come sleep with me yes and he knows that too at the bottom of his heart take that Mrs Maybrick that poisoned her husband for what I wonder in love with some other man yes it was found out on her wasnt she the downright villain to go and do a thing like that of course some men can be dreadfully aggravating drive you mad and always the worst word in the world what do they ask us to marry them for if were so bad as all that comes to yes because they cant get on without us white Arsenic she put in his tea off flypaper wasnt it I wonder why they call it that if I asked him hed say its from the Greek leave us as wise as we were before she must have been madly in love with the other fellow to run the chance of being hanged O she didn't care if that was her nature what could she do besides theyre not brutes enough to go and hang a woman surely are they [. . .]

(Joyce 1960 [1922]: 880)

Molly Bloom's thoughts are given in a rush of consciousness, in which we can discern some coherence. She grumbles to herself about her husband and men, and matrimony in general. Her thoughts about husband-poisoner Mrs Maybrick veer from conventional disgust to fascination and sneaking sympathy.

The advantage of this method is that it can seem very authentic and alive. It has been influential in the way that writers now render subjectivity, trying to capture the fluid nature of thought processes, though this is usually done nowadays in a modified form, with punctuation. This is because untrammelled stream of consciousness can slow narrative pace since it is inevitably rambling and unfocused. But it can be an effective technique to use in short bursts, particularly for rants, intoxicated states of mind, or traumatised moments.

Activity 6.7   Writing

Take the situation of a clown putting on make-up before an illuminated mirror. He has just been evicted from his flat. Write up to 250 words of his thoughts, using stream of consciousness. You may omit punctuation if you like or use some as in this example: 'Now for the application of big red lips. I see red I see red I see red. Show must go on. Show nothing to punters . . .'

Voice: tone and attitude

Whatever point of view you choose, it will deliver a particular voice. A convincing narrative voice is a crucial element in achieving the distinctive tone of a piece of fiction.

Writers often feel daunted about the possibility of writing anything original. Everything about the human condition has already been beautifully said. There have been billions of births, bereavements and betrayals in the world, and there is nothing new under the sun. But when something big happens to *you*, it feels new and personal. It is this freshness of experience, no matter how 'commonplace', that can be captured by creating an individual voice for a piece of fiction.

Activity 6.8   Reading

To see the impact of dramatically different narrative voices on the same theme, let's look at the openings of Rick Moody's *Purple America* and Andrew Miller's *Oxygen*.

- What is the shared theme?
- Which point of view has each author chosen?
- How would you describe the narrative voices in each?

Extract 1

Whosoever knows the folds and complexities of his own mother's body, *he shall never die*. Whosoever knows the latitudes of his mother's body, whosoever has taken her into his arms and immersed her baptismally in the first-floor tub, lifting one of her alabaster legs and then the other over its lip, whosoever bathes her with Woolworth's soaps in sample sizes, whosoever twists the creaky taps and tests the water on the inside of his wrist, who-soever shovels a couple of tablespoons of rose bath salts under the billowing faucet and marvels at their vermilion color, whosoever bends by hand her sclerotic limbs, as if reassuring himself about the condition of a hinge, whosoever has kissed his mother on the part that separates the lobes of her white hair and has cooed her name while soaping underneath the breast where he was once fed, whosoever breathes the acrid and dispiriting stench of his mother's body while scrubbing the greater part of this smell away with Woolworth's lavender soaps, who has pushed her discarded bra and oversized panties (scattered on the tile floor behind him) to one side, away from the water sloshing occasionally over the edge of the tub and choking the runoff drain, who has lost his footing on these panties, panties once dotted with blood of children unconceived, his siblings unconceived, panties now intended to fit over a vinyl undergarment, who has wiped stalactites of drool from his mother's mouth with a moistened violet washcloth, who has swept back the annoying violet shower curtain the better to lift up his stick-figure mother and to bathe her ass, where a sweet and infantile shit sometimes collects, causing her both discomfort and shame, whosoever angrily manhandles the dial on the bathroom radio (balanced on the toilet tank) with one wet hand in an effort to find a college station that blasts only compact disc recordings of train accidents and large-scale construction operations (*he should be over this noise by his age*), whosoever selects at last the drummers of Burundi on WUCN knowing full well that his mother can brook only the music of the Tin Pan Alley period and certain classics, and whosoever has then reacted guiltily to his own selfishness and tuned to some lite AM station featuring the greatest hits of swing, whosoever will notice in the course of his mission the ripe light of early November as it is played out on the wall of the bathroom where one of those plug-in electric candles with plastic base is the only source of illumination, whosoever waits in this half-light while his mother takes her last bodily pleasure: the time in which her useless body floats in the warm, humid, even lapping of rose-scented bathwater, a water which in spite of its pleasures occasionally causes in his mother transient scotoma, ataxia, difficulty swallowing, deafness, and other temporary dysfunctions consistent with her ailment, whosoever looks nonetheless at his pacific mom's face in that water and knows — in a New Age kind of way — the face he had before he was born, whosoever weeps over his mother's condition while bathing her, silently weeps, without words or expressions of pity or any nose-blowing or honking while crying, just weeps for a second like a ninny, whosoever has thereafter recovered quickly and forcefully from despair, whosoever has formulated a simple gratitude for the fact that *he still has a mother*, but who has nonetheless wondered at the kind of astral justice that has immobilized her thus, whosoever has then wished that the bath was over already so that he could go and drink too much at a local bar, a bar where he will encounter the citizens of this his hometown, a bar where he will see his cronies from high school, those who never left, those who have stayed to become civic boosters, those who have sent kids to the same day school they themselves attended thirty years before [. . .]

(Moody 1998: 3, 4)

Extract 2

She was not asleep when he went in. She lay propped against the pillows in her nightgown and quilted robe, reading a book. The room was very warm. The heat of the sun was in the timbers of the roof, and the radiator was on high, so that everything sweated its particular smell, a stuffiness half intimate, half medical, that hung in the air like a sediment. Vases of cut flowers, some from the garden, some from friends, added a note of hothouse sweetness, and there was a perfume she sprayed as a kind of luxurious air-freshener, which masked very little, but which Alec could always taste in his mouth for an hour after leaving the room.

Cleanliness – even the illusion of it – was an obsession with her now, as though the sickness were something, some lapse in hygiene, that might be hidden behind veils of scent. For an hour each morning and evening she washed herself with catlike attention in the en-suite bathroom, the only real physical work she still did. But no soaps or night creams or lavender shower gel could entirely hide what filtered out from the disasters inside of her, though nothing would ever be quite as disturbing as that first course of chemotherapy the winter of two years ago, when she had sat wrapped in picnic rugs on the sofa in the living room, alien and wretched and smelling like a child's chemistry set. When her hair had grown again, it had sprouted brilliant white, and was now a weight of frost-coloured locks that reached to the mid-point of her back. (. . .)

'Everything all right, Mum?' He was standing just inside the door, hands in pockets, very slightly rocking on the balls of his feet.

'Fine, dear.'

'Need anything?'

She shook her head.

'Sure?'

'Thank you, dear.'

'Cup of tea?'

'No, thank you.'

'I've done the garden.'

'Good.'

'How about some hot milk?'

'No, thank you.'

'You haven't forgotten your Zopiclone?'

'No, dear, I haven't. Do try not to fuss.'

She frowned at him, the old headmistress again, bothered by some wittering pupil. A go-away look.

'I'll let you read,' he said. 'Look in later.'

She nodded, the movement triggering off a fit of coughing, but as he moved towards her (what was he going to *do*?) she waved him away and he went out, listening from the landing until she was quiet, then going slowly down the stairs, blushing from an emotion he could not quite identify.

(Miller 2001: 12–14)

Discussion

Both stories are about the anguished sons of ailing mothers. They reflect the common plight of adult offspring having to come to terms with a parent's dying. The opening chapter of *Oxygen* uses a third-person limited viewpoint, bringing us close to Alec, the younger son. *Purple America* has an omniscient narrator who even uses one of the 'old-fashioned' devices of omniscience when he concludes with a final moral verdict in praise of carers: 'And if he's a hero, then heroes are five-and-dime, and the world is as crowded with them as it is with stray pets, worn tires, and missing keys' (Moody 1998: 7).

The voices could hardly be more different. *Purple America* opens with a deliberately dazzling piece of rhetoric. It has one unbroken four-page sentence, about half of which is shown above. The sentence rises to a crescendo through the use of anaphora, the repetition of the same word at the beginning of successive clauses for rhetorical effect. As 'whosoever' is a word hijacked from the New Testament promise of victory over death ['Whosoever believeth in me, he shall never die.' (John 11, 26)], this creates a kind of transgressive liturgy in which the narrator is claiming a sacramental value for the rituals of caring for an elderly parent. The voice is rousing and provocative, full of wit, rage, and tenderness. Ultimately, in his praise of carers everywhere, the narrator moves out from the almost unbearably intimate scene.

By contrast, *Oxygen* has a very restrained tone in keeping with the reticent coping behaviour of both mother and son. This understatement makes their powerlessness, their inability to comfort one another, all the more piercing.

The effects of both pieces – stunningly tender and transgressive; or muted and moving – emerge from their respective authors' decisions about point of view and voice.

Conclusion

The critical element of any point of view is the narrative voice, a defining tone or attitude which filters through the story. Here is a summary of what this entails in relation to the viewpoints explored in this chapter and the preceding one:

- With a first-person narrator, the voice will be that character's distinctive language and phraseology, his or her way of thinking and writing.
- With second-person narration, the 'you' includes the reader as a player in the unfolding story or refers to the main character's divided self.
- With third-person limited omniscience, there will be a combination of the main character's personal voice and the narrator's reporting of that in free indirect style.
- With multiple viewpoints in the third person, there will be a subtle shift of tone each time you enter a different character's point of view.
- With third-person objective, the voice will be in a dispassionate tone, offering no interpretation of the events witnessed.
- With full omniscience, the tone will reveal the persona of your storyteller: majestic, barnstorming, forensic, elegiac, witty, unassuming, whatever you decide.

127

It requires practice to 'get' these various methods, so do refer back to the examples given. Also study the manipulation of point of view in every fiction you read, making notes in your notebook about strategies that impress you and that you would like to try.

References

Barker, Pat (1999) *Another World*, London: Penguin.

Chekhov, Anton (1964 [1899]) *Lady with Lapdog and Other Stories*, David Margarshack (tr.), London: Penguin.

Hemingway, Ernest (1993), *The Essential Hemingway*, London: Arrow Books.

Hodgkinson, Amanda (no date) *The Tree House*, manuscript (unpublished).

Joyce, James (1960 [1922]) *Ulysses*, London: The Bodley Head.

Kincaid, Jamaica (1983) *At the Bottom of the River*, New York: Farrar Straus Giroux.

Lodge, David (2003 [2002]) *Consciousness and the Novel*, London: Penguin Books.

Lott, Tim (2003) *Rumours of a Hurricane*, London: Penguin.

McGahern, John (1983 [1965]) *The Dark*, London: Faber & Faber.

Miller, Andrew (2001) *Oxygen*, London: Sceptre.

Moody, Rick (1998) *Purple America*, London: Flamingo.

Woolf, Virginia (1987 [1949]) *Lappin and Lapinova* in Hermione Lee (ed.) *The Secret Self 2: Short stories by women*, Everyman's Library, London: J.M. Dent & Sons.

7

Showing and telling

Derek Neale

What are showing and telling?

Having created a character or three, established a setting, and generally got the story moving, the new writer is often then given technical advice, such as 'show don't tell'. Yet what does this apparently simple instruction mean? On one level 'show don't tell' would seem an easy rule to follow. In practical terms it means that instead of writing 'He was angry' you describe the way 'He screwed the piece of paper into a tight ball and threw it so hard it bounced off the wall and the table before landing back at his feet.'

This is certainly one version of what is meant, but 'show don't tell' is an instruction that is interpreted and intended in a number of subtly different ways. In this chapter you will see different illustrations of what 'showing' and 'telling' might mean in practice.

The terms 'showing' and 'telling' first surfaced at the turn of the nine-teenth to twentieth century, in the writings of Henry James and Percy Lubbock. James, reputedly in a margin note on one of his drafts, urged himself to 'Dramatize! Dramatize! Dramatize! (James 1948: 265). Percy Lubbock, a critic at the time, interpreted this as an exhortation for novelists to 'show don't tell', and developed it into a prescription for how 'good fiction' should be written:

The art of fiction does not begin until the novelist thinks of his story as a matter to be shown, to be so exhibited that it will tell itself.'

(Lubbock 1963: 62)

Lubbock went on to criticise novelists whose narrators were too intrusive – nineteenth-century novelists such as Thackeray and Dickens, for instance. A more moderate and all-embracing view of how fiction is written has appeared since, with modern commentators assessing the methods of both showing and telling. For instance, in his book *The Rhetoric of Fiction* (1991) Wayne C. Booth argues that all narratives operate using degrees of showing and telling – it is impossible to tell a story without including some dramatisation and some summary.

This debate is important, because you will always be deploying a relative degree of 'showing' and 'telling' in your fiction. You will often need to look at the balance between the two. Sometimes you will have to cover events quickly because the small detail of those events will not be relevant to your story; sometimes you will have to pause and ponder over events because those particulars will be of great significance either to the character or your story in general – but most pertinently for your reader.

Activity 7.1 Reading

Read the following extract from the essay by Lindsay Clarke, 'Going the Last Inch: Some thoughts on showing and telling'. In particular, write down in your notebook your responses to these questions:

- What is the difference between the two versions of 'crying' talked about by Clarke, especially in relation to time?
- What are the problems of showing too little and too much?

In the early drafts of a piece, you are still working out what you are trying to say to yourself, and too much mental trafficking with an audience at that stage can inhibit the flow of your imagination. But if you mean to go public, then sooner or later you have to consider the legitimate needs of your readers, and a large part of the process of revision will be about making sure that you have given their imagination all the room it needs to work [. . .] To understand why, you need only ask which is more immediately engaging – to witness an event for yourself or to be told about it afterwards by someone else?

A brief example will *show* what the distinction between showing and telling can mean for fiction. If, in a first novel, an author had written, 'The boy broke down and began to cry so wretchedly that the other small children started howling too,' he would, rather dully, have told us something. When, in *The Lord of the Flies*, William Golding wrote that 'his face puckered, the tears leapt from his eyes, his mouth opened till they could see a square black hole . . . The crying went on, breath after breath, and seemed to sustain him upright as if he were nailed to it,' he has unforgettably *shown* us something. By which I mean that he has brought us so closely into the presence of the weeping child that we can see him and hear him and feel our own inconsolable portion in the sense of universal grief he disturbs in the other 'littluns'. Who could prefer the told version to the shown? [. . .]

[Yet] if we insist on showing everything, especially things that might more effectively be told, then it won't be long before we start to bore the reader. The error shows itself in the common tendency of young writers to begin in the wrong place, so that we must watch the leading character get out of bed, stare in the mirror, eat breakfast and so on, to the point where we begin to lose interest long before some intriguing encounter seizes our attention. In those dull circumstances, the collaboration with the reader will end before it's properly got started. So what seems to be in question is the right choice of narrative strategy *at any given moment*. Do I tell the readers this or should I show it? Which approach will most effectively draw them into the dream of the novel, and keep them there till the dream is done?

In practice this means hunting down those moments that unintentionally tip the reader out of the dream. They can be considered under two broad headings: problems that arise from underwriting, when the author hasn't done enough imaginative work to secure the collaboration of the reader, and those of overwriting, when the reader is crowded out by the author trying to do too much.

Merely telling the reader something that's crying out to be dramatized is a form of underwriting. William Blake once wrote that 'he who does not imagine in minute particulars does not imagine at all', and it seems clear that if we don't bring the focused energy of the imagination to bear on the scene we're writing, then we're unlikely to activate its full potential for exciting the reader's interest.

(Clarke 2001: 256–58)

Discussion

It's important to notice the equal emphasis given to both showing and telling: they each have their uses. Following on from James's exhortation ('Dramatize, dramatize, dramatize'), showing is often equated with a writing method that dramatises; telling is often seen as a writing method that summarises. Showing in this sense can be seen as a type of writing which unpacks the detail of a scene or episode; telling by contrast is a type of writing which tends to pass more fleetingly over the details.

The Golding passage, for instance where the crying goes on 'breath after breath', seems to unpack the action of crying, to stretch time, so the moment is expanded and more fully matches the significance of the tears. As Clarke suggests, showing and telling are relative methods. When you write 'he cried' it is in effect showing the emotional state of sadness in action, but it has only gone one step away from that abstract state, to a first basic action. It is a very brief summation of what the real life state of being sad usually entails. It hasn't attempted to imitate the duration of the crying or sadness.

Real time and fictional time are rarely aligned, but there is a proportionate relationship. Sometimes it will be appropriate to say 'he cried'; sometimes it will be necessary to spend longer with the scene, to breathe life into the moments of crying, the actual detail, the internal thoughts, and perhaps the causes and consequences. Remember that at climactic moments, fictional time can expand and have an even longer duration than the equivalent 'real' event.

Showing

Sometimes you will have to cover events quickly because the small detail of those events will not be relevant to your story; sometimes you will have to pause over events because those particulars will be of great significance, either to the character or your story in general. You can improve the veracity of your writing and increase the amount of showing in it by watching out for adjectives that are too general, and by guarding against the overuse of adverbs. When you find that you have used a cliché, be honest about it and admit that you may have fallen asleep momentarily when writing that line. It happens to us all. It is to be expected but it is a fault that can and should be addressed. Clichés are often a sign that you are telling too much. This is what Clarke says later in his essay:

> Watch out for a reliance on abstract nouns in your writing, particularly those to do with states of feeling. Simply to announce that a character is 'filled with fury' or 'rotten with jealousy' is the weakest way to make your reader feel the impact of their emotions. We have your word for it but little else. However, if you show us the children wincing as Harriet throws the curry she's just cooked across the kitchen, or we see Ken straining to overhear a telephone call through a closed door, then we draw our own conclusions. It's a useful exercise to forbid yourself the use of keynote words such as 'fury' or 'jealous' when dramatizing an emotional condition. Similarly, when you find yourself writing *about* an important conversation, ask whether your readers might not prefer to hear the exchanges for themselves, particularly as characters are revealed through the different ways they use the language, and dialogue can subtly move the narrative along. [. . .] If you don't care enough about the characters and events of your story to do them imaginative justice, why should the reader stay inside the dream [of the novel]?
>
> Overwriting indicates a failure to trust the imagination of the reader. Consider how much of the pleasure of reading comes from inferring that which has nowhere been explicitly stated. A writer who pre-empts such moments of realization by obtrusive winks and nudges soon becomes a bore. The same is true of any lack of economy and concision in your prose. By making a careful selection of details from a scene that you've imagined for yourself 'in minute particulars', you free your readers to visualize it too. But if you pile on the adjectives, or double the contents of your sentences through the loose use of similes, you are more likely to crowd them out.
>
> Often enough you'll find that less can do more.
>
> (Clarke 2001: 258–260)

Avoiding abstractions

Telling, as Clarke suggests, sometimes summarises abstract emotions – such as love, sadness, or happiness – in a way that doesn't quite satisfy the reader. There are times when it will be appropriate to write 'She was irate' or 'He was sad', but there will be times when your reader will need more: they will need to see the crunched up paper bouncing off the walls; they will want to see your characters laughing or crying, and to be interpreting events for themselves.

Activity 7.2   Writing

'He was sad', if shown, might become: 'His shoulders heaved and he let out a long, frail sigh as he turned towards the door.'

'She was irate', if shown, might become: 'She glared through him, past him, stabbing the desk with her pencil.'

Using these as examples, for each of the statements below containing an emotional or physical state, write one or two sentences showing it in action:

- He felt tired.
- She loved him.
- They loathed one another.
- The children were bored.
- Grandmother came home drunk.

Discussion

As soon as you ask questions about how to bring a particular state to life, you also ask questions about who he was or who she was, and what might have made them tired or bored or whatever. You then start picturing scenarios and inventing details about the characters. Your reader will be doing this too. They feed off every scrap of information you give them, and soon become actively involved in recreating the causes and consequences of events.

In this way showing generates more vivid sensory pictures and arouses a more pressing intrigue than telling. You might show the grandmother falling over and the reader will be immediately intrigued. Why is she falling over? Is she ill? Has she been drinking? Why has she been drinking? Does she always do this? Did something happen that caused her to get drunk? You may not have got as far as answering these questions in your one or two sentences, but it is important to remember that this is the way the reader is working, and most readers like being active in the story in this fashion.

The role of your reader

Readers want to be involved; they want to ask questions and like to use their imagination in providing some of the answers themselves. If you give your reader too quick and full a summary of events you disengage their creativity and run the serious risk of sending them to sleep. David Lodge suggests that 'A novel written entirely in the mode of summary would [. . .] be almost unreadable' (Lodge 1992: 122). Certainly if you have a predominance of telling in your writing, your style might veer towards reportage. Yet telling is importantly used to speed up the tempo, 'rushing us through events which would be uninteresting or *too* interesting – therefore distracting, if lingered over' (Lodge 1992: 122).

For instance, in a simple passage of summary such as 'They went to the park and he said to her that it was going to be okay', we get the basic information about location, participants and what happened, all conveyed in matter-of-fact fashion, via the voice of the narrator.

In a 'shown' version of the same episode there would be more detail and it would be dramatised. It might read like this:

> The lights from the road reached the children's slide, but the swings where they were sitting were in almost complete dark. A dog sauntered past, sniffing briefly before running back off towards the road. The wind got up.
>
> 'It will be alright you know,' he said.
>
> 'Yeah,' she said, her hair falling over her eyes.
>
> 'No, really – it will be alright.'
>
> 'I said okay, didn't I,' she said, pushing off and swinging high into the starless night.

The information about the wind, the dog, the dark and the road provide a much fuller picture, as does the dialogue. The reader might even be delving into what isn't being said and starting to invent the dynamic between the two characters. If the incident in the park is an insignificant part of the story then all this detail and the level of invention, on the part of writer and reader, would be wasted and, what's more, misleading. The reader would be looking for significance where there was none.

Activity 7.3   Writing

Bearing in mind the scene in the park as an example, write a 'shown' version (using up to 100 words) of one of the following sentences:

- He went to see his father to make arrangements to move the furniture.
- They were all together in one room and she felt tired and claustrophobic.
- She waited with her sister, drinking tea, seeking reassurance.
- Back at the office the solicitor called with a new piece of evidence that had come to light.

Discussion

Showing doesn't mean that you include all possible detail, but rather the pertinent detail. The scene in the park, for instance, includes the details about light and dark because that echoes the uneasy state between the two characters. Similarly, the dog's quick departure signals the unfriendly and private nature of the scene. When attempting to 'show' in this fashion, try to be concise and don't include unnecessary information. If you found that you went over the word limit, go back and cut. When editing, always ask the questions: 'Have I shown too much?' and 'Do I need to show that?'

When you get time, write in your notebook a 'shown' version for the three sentences that you didn't pick.

Telling

But what about stories where telling dominates? We will now look at a story from *Tales from the Thousand and One Nights*, a collection of ancient stories written in Arabic, first introduced into Europe in the early eighteenth century and often translated thereafter. The framework is that the Sultan Schahriah has each of his wives strangled on the morning after the consummation of their marriage. However, one of his wives, the clever young Scheherazade, amuses him for a thousand and one nights by telling him tales, as a result of which he revokes his cruel decree. One of the most famous sequences in the collection concerns the adventures of Sinbad the Sailor. The story we are going to look at is called 'The Dream'.

Activity 7.4   Reading

Read 'The Dream', below.

As you read, in your notebook write down:

- any elements of the story that 'show' rather than 'tell';
- any elements of the story that 'tell';
- how time is handled in the story.

The Dream

There lived once in Baghdad a merchant who, having squandered all his wealth, became so destitute that he could make his living only by the hardest labour.

One night he lay down to sleep with a heavy heart, and in a dream a man appeared to him, saying: 'Your fortune lies in Cairo. Go and seek it there.'

The very next morning he set out for Cairo and, after many weeks and much hardship on the way, arrived in that city. Night had fallen, and as he could not afford to stay at an inn he lay down to sleep in the courtyard of a mosque.

Now as the Almighty's will would have it, a band of robbers entered the mosque and from there broke into an adjoining house. Awakened by the noise, the owners raised the alarm and shouted for help; then the thieves made off. Presently the Chief of Police and his men arrived on the scene. They entered the mosque and, finding the man from Baghdad lying in the courtyard, seized him and beat him with their clubs until he was nearly dead. Then they threw him into prison.

Three days later the Chief of Police ordered his men to bring the stranger before him.

'Where do you come from?' asked the chief.

'From Baghdad.'

'And what has brought you to Cairo?'

'A man appeared to me in a dream, saying: "Your fortune lies in Cairo. Go and seek it there." But when I came to Cairo, the fortune I was promised proved to be the blows your men so generously gave me.'

When he heard this, the Chief of Police burst out laughing. 'Know then, you fool,' he cried, 'that I too have heard a voice in my sleep, not just once but on three occasions. It said: "Go to Baghdad, and in a cobbled street lined with palm trees you will find such-and-such a house, with a courtyard of grey marble; at the far end of the garden there is a fountain of white marble. Under the fountain a great sum of money lies buried. Go there and dig it up." But would I go? Of course not. Yet, fool that you are, you have come all the way to Cairo on the strength of one idle dream.'

Then the Chief of Police gave the merchant some money. 'Here,' he said, 'take this. It will help you on the way back to your own country.'

The merchant recognized at once that the house and garden just described were his own. He took the money and set out promptly on his homeward journey.

As soon as he reached his house he went into the garden, dug beneath the fountain, and uncovered a great treasure.

Thus the words of the dream were wondrously fulfilled, and Allah made the ruined merchant rich again.

(Anon, N. J. Dawood (trans) 1973: 328–9)

Discussion

In terms of time and place this story never seems to pause. Swathes of time are covered – the merchant travels from Baghdad to Cairo in the blink of an eye; he sleeps through a robbery, which is summarised in a sentence. Yet there are some shown elements, for instance when characters speak. Note, though, that even here the exchanges have no real setting. All we know is that it is 'three days later' when the policeman talks to the merchant; we don't get the co-ordinates of a fully dramatised scene – a description of the room, what the characters looked like, or what they may have been thinking. The way in which time is quickly summarised – three days passing in a single clause of a sentence – seems typical of the way time operates in the narrative.

Exposition

You might have found 'The Dream' to be like a fairy story or parable. Such stories seem to have some other purpose than realising the particular details of a world. They operate in a simple, linear fashion, starting from point A and going straight to point B then C. Their respective plots dominate, suggesting that the overall shape and combination of events is more important than the small detail. The characters are types rather than real people. In 'The Dream', for instance, the main character is just 'a merchant'; he isn't even given a name.

These are perhaps not the sort of characters you wish to create in your fiction, but you can still use such summary techniques to help realise your peripheral characters or action, and to develop your main character, for instance, by giving them some history, what is sometimes called 'back-story'. Showing everything you know about your characters is neither possible nor desirable. Some information will be best left to summary.

One version of the fiction writing process has it that writing is all about information – withholding it and disclosing it. The writer is always doing one or the other – either keeping things unknown or drip-feeding the reader with details. Revealing information about certain aspects of your story is often termed 'exposition' – you are exposing the flesh and bones of it, what has happened, what is happening, what might happen. Ursula Le Guin suggests that all narratives carry some explanatory and descriptive load and that you can learn the skill of handling this 'expository freight' by making the information part of the story. For Le Guin, as for many other writers, the craft lies in breaking the exposition into small deposits so it doesn't come out as a lecture or an 'expository lump' (Le Guin 1998: 119).

When writing summary passages that apparently 'tell' a lot, it's important to remember that they should also be leaving a lot out. Some of this omitted information will be irrelevant, but some of it can be the sort of detail that, by its very omission, will keep your reader awake and active. So, a summary of the drunken grandmother's backstory, for instance, might cover the fact that she has been drinking for twenty years, that she especially likes a certain kind of malt whisky, that she has two sons and five grandchildren, that she is divorced but still on amicable terms with her former husband, and that she once had a daughter. But this summary might then exclude crucial details about why the grandmother 'once had' a daughter. Has the daughter been disowned? Is the daughter dead? Was there an argument and did the daughter leave home? Was this the cause of the drinking? The reader still needs to be asking questions when you are in telling mode; it should never be an excuse to overwrite or to give too much information.

You might use a telling technique when your narrative needs to move quickly in terms of location or time; between different eras of a character's life, for instance, or when they move from place to place. In most cases you might not want to detail the intervening action and events, but need nonetheless to make the reader aware of the shift. So, the story of the drunken grandmother might cover ten years, culminating in a reunion with her errant daughter. It would be impossible to 'show' all of the intervening years, so you 'tell' just significant details, establish the passage of time, as with the merchant going to and from Cairo in 'The Dream'.

Activity 7.5   Writing

Picking a character either from your notebook or one you encountered and worked on in Activity 7.2 or 7.3, write a brief passage of backstory connected to the character. In your summary include a movement in time - the passing of years or days. Write up to 200 words.

Dialogue and stories

Writers have often experimented with the balance between showing and telling. Ernest Hemingway wrote many stories in which the summary narrative is pared down and the dialogue is dominant and carries the story forward. In his story 'Hills Like White Elephants', which involves a man and a woman in Spain, waiting at a bar for a train, there is very little description. What scene-setting there is appears at the start of the story, in an opening paragraph. The subsequent three pages of the narrative consist almost totally of dialogue between the two characters. It is a tense conversation but one which never breaks out into an argument. Many of the lines conceal meaning, and it is an exchange in which the reader works hard to decipher the subtext and underlying dynamic between the characters. This is typified by the way they talk of the central topic of their exchange – the woman's imminent abortion. This is never named but is called 'it' throughout. This is the woman starting a section of the dialogue:

'If I do it you won't ever worry?'

'I won't worry about that because it's perfectly simple.'

'Then I'll do it. Because I don't care about me.'

'What do you mean?'

'I don't care about me.'

'Well, I care about you.'

'Oh, yes. But I don't care about me. And I'll do it and then everything will be fine.'

(Hemingway 1995 [1927]: 201)

You can see from this that many things do not get said, though the lines of dialogue are always giving the reader clues as to the characters' hidden feelings. The reader's imagination is very active in such a story. The dialogue is predominant but there are still odd lines of necessary description:

The girl stood up and walked to the end of the station. Across, on the other side, were fields of grain and trees along the banks of the Ebro. Far away, beyond the river were mountains. The shadow of a cloud moved across the field of grain and she saw the river through the trees.

(Hemingway 1995 [1927]: 201)

These little passages, of which there are very few in the story, help to link the physical components of the scene to the voices. Another Hemingway story, 'Today is Friday' (Hemingway 1995 [1927]: 268–271) about two Roman soldiers at the time of Christ's crucifixion, is written totally in dialogue. It looks like a dramatic script, though it is published as a short story. Similarly, Katherine Mansfield wrote a story called 'The Black Cap', about a woman about to leave her husband but having second thoughts. The story attempts to dispense with telling altogether, by writing the narrative details in the form of stage directions; the rest of the story is written in dialogue. Let's have a closer look at how she did it.

Activity 7.6   Reading

Read the following extract from Katherine Mansfield's 'The Black Cap' and note

- how location and characters are realised;
- how the dialogue moves the story forward.

> (*A lady and her husband are seated at breakfast. He is quite calm, reading the newspaper and eating; but she is strangely excited, dressed for travelling, and only pretending to eat.*)
>
> SHE: Oh, if you should want your flannel shirts, they are on the right-hand bottom shelf of the linen press.
>
> HE: (*at a board meeting of the Meat Export Company*): No.
>
> SHE: You didn't hear what I said. I said if you should want your flannel shirts, they are on the right-hand bottom shelf of the linen press.
>
> HE: (*positively*): I quite agree!
>
> SHE: It does seem rather extraordinary that on the very morning that I am going away you cannot leave the newspaper alone for five minutes.
>
> HE (*mildly*): My dear woman, I don't want you to go. In fact, I have asked you not to go. I can't for the life of me see. . . .
>
> SHE: You know perfectly well that I am only going because I absolutely must. I've been putting it off and putting it off, and the dentist said last time. . . .
>
> HE: Good! Good! Don't let's go all over the ground again. We've thrashed it all out pretty thoroughly, haven't we?
>
> SERVANT: Cab's here, m'm.
>
> SHE: Please put my luggage in.
>
> SERVANT: Very good, m'm.
>
> (*She gives a tremendous sigh.*)

(Mansfield 1984: 207–9)

Discussion

You might find that this stage script method seems strange because it isn't a conventional way of presenting dialogue in a story. It has, however, been used by other writers in sections of their novels – Samuel

Richardson in *Clarissa* (1985 [1748]), James Joyce in *Ulysses* (1960 [1922]), and more recently Andrew O'Hagan in *Personality* (2003). The more widely known methods for presenting dialogue might place the speech within quotation marks and accompany the lines with a reporting clause (often called 'tags') – he said, she said, he asked, she replied. These clauses are sometimes left out, if the identity of the speaker is well established, and usually when the dialogue involves just two characters. It can get confusing otherwise. Whatever method of presenting dialogue you use, it is important for your reader that the identity of a speaker is unambiguous, and that your method is consistent throughout each individual story. You can see in 'The Black Cap' that the material details and actions of the story are given very briefly. Most of the narrative information has to be inferred from the dialogue. It is not long though before you get an idea of each individual character's way of speaking. From the way that they talk and what they say the reader quickly develops a picture of events.

Activity 7.7   Writing

Take a particular moment from 'The Dream' and write it as a 'play script' story, as in 'The Black Cap'. Concentrate on just one sentence of the original story and produce only a brief adaptation (up to 200 words). When you have finished, in your notebook write some reflections on the following:

- what you consider to be the elements you lose by using this method compared to a more conventional narrative;
- what you consider to be gained.

Discussion

As soon as you begin inhabiting the characters and pausing over a dramatic event you start thinking about the story slightly differently. Showing events in this way may well mean that the story becomes different altogether. One of the potential gains from realising events through showing is the dramatic energy it harnesses in bringing the characters to life. However, you may have missed the power of description: the potential of certain details related to place and character, together with sensory details, to reveal the story.

'The Dream' contains no interior narrative about characters' thoughts. In adapting part of it you may have wondered how this might be achieved. Revealing a character's thoughts in a story is a powerful tool in helping you to portray that character. Character thoughts can also help to move the story along. Mansfield achieves this to a certain extent in 'The Black Cap' by including various monologues for the woman. This is her monologue on the way to the station after she has left her husband:

> SHE: How strange life is! I didn't think I should feel like this at all. All the glamour seems to have gone, somehow. Oh, I'd give anything for the cab to turn round and go back. The most curious thing is that I feel if he really had made me believe he loved me it would have been much easier to have left him. But that's absurd. How strong the hay smells. It's going to be a very hot day. I shall never see these fields again. Never, never! But in another way I am glad that it happened like this; it puts me so finally, absolutely in the right for ever! He doesn't want a woman at all. A woman has no meaning for him. He's not the type of man to care deeply for anybody except himself. I've become the person who remembers to take the links out of his shirts before they go to the wash – that is all! And that's not enough for me. I'm young – I'm too proud. I'm not the type of woman to vegetate in the country and rave over 'our' own lettuces. . . . What you have been trying to do, ever since you married me is to make me submit, to turn me into your shadow, to rely on me so utterly that you'd only to glance up to find the right time printed on me somehow, as if I were a clock. You have never been curious about me; you never wanted to explore my soul. No; you wanted me to settle down to your peaceful existence. Oh! how your blindness has outraged me – how I hate you for it! I am glad – thankful – thankful to have left you!

(Mansfield 1984: 209)

The woman is given further monologues during the course of the story, charting how her thoughts eventually turn against the prospect of leaving her husband – she returns home in the end in time for tea. Monologues and soliloquies are the way in which stage plays usually achieve the sense of a character's interior life, and you can sometimes use the methods of stage drama to achieve the same effect. The narrative voice of a novel or short story is very similar to the voice in a dramatic monologue. Both have the potential to reveal intimate thoughts.

Mixing drama and summary

Mansfield's 'The Black Cap' is an extreme example of how a story might be written using dramatic methods, mostly in dialogue. More usually you will deploy a mixed method, one which incorporates some dialogue with some passages of summary and description. Even in stories which appear to rely heavily on dialogue and which are predominantly dramatised – such as Hemingway's 'Hills Like White Elephants' - there is a fine balance between 'shown' and 'told' elements. Some parts of the story are still revealed through summary – such as the description of location and characters' actions. This balance between showing and telling will vary according to the writer and the demands of a particular story.

The short story 'The Dying Room' by Georgina Hammick is about a conversation in a kitchen between a mother and her adult son. It begins like this:

I think I left my wireless in the drawing room, his mother said. Could you get it? I'd be grateful.

His mother and he were in the kitchen. He took a big breath. He said, You can't use that word any more, I'm sorry, we've decided.

What word are you talking about? his mother said. She took a tray of cheese tartlets from the oven and put them on the table. His mother is a cook. She cooks for her family when they're at home and she cooks professionally: for other women's freezers and other women's lunch and dinner parties. She also supplies, on a regular basis, her local delicatessen with pâtés and terrines and tarts and quiches. Blast, these look a bit burnt to me, his mother said. Do they look burnt to you? What word can't I use?

'Drawing room', he said. It's an anachronism, it's irrelevant. It's snobbish. It has associations with mindless West End theatre. It's embarrassing.

His mother said nothing for a minute. She looked thoughtful; she looked thoughtfully at her feet. Then she said, Who are 'we'? 'We' who have decided?

My sisters and I, he told her. Your children. All of them.

145

I see, his mother said. First I've heard of this, I have to say.

The point is, he said, our friends, the ones we bring here, find it offensive – or a joke. And so do we. It is offensive, and ridiculous, to continue to use a word that means nothing to ninety-nine per cent of the population, that ninety-nine per cent of the population does not use.

(Hammick 1996: 368)

This story is largely made up of direct speech. Curiously it presents this using the reporting clauses – he said, she said – but it omits the quotation marks. The use of dialogue and the dramatic scene is its showing method, though it has some telling passages too – for instance when the mother's occupation of cook is summarised early on, so giving the reader background to the character. Such passages tend to be brief and isolated, but, as will be seen in the next chapter, have a crucial effect on the structure of the story. Now let's look at another story which appears to do a lot of showing but which also reveals itself through telling.

Activity 7.8 Reading

Read 'I could see the smallest things' by Raymond Carver, below.
   Write in your notebook:

- any elements of showing and what these give to the story;
- any elements of telling and what these give to the story.

I could see the smallest things

I was in bed when I heard the gate. I listened carefully. I didn't hear anything else. But I heard that. I tried to wake Cliff. He was passed out. So I got up and went to the window. A big moon was laid over the mountains that went around the city. It was a white moon and covered with scars. Any damn fool could imagine a face there.

There was light enough so that I could see everything in the yard – lawn chairs, the willow tree, clothesline strung between the poles, the petunias, the fences, the gate standing wide open.

But nobody was moving around. There were no scary shadows. Everything lay in moonlight, and I could see the smallest things. The clothespins on the line, for instance.

I put my hands on the glass to block out the moon. I looked some more. I listened. Then I went back to bed.

But I couldn't get to sleep. I kept turning over. I thought about the gate standing open. It was like a dare.

Cliff's breathing was awful to listen to. His mouth gaped open and his arms hugged his pale chest. He was taking up his side of the bed and most of mine.

I pushed and pushed on him. But he just groaned.

I stayed still awhile longer until I decided it was no use. I got up and got my slippers. I went to the kitchen and made tea and sat with it at the kitchen table. I smoked one of Cliff's unfiltereds.

It was late. I didn't want to look at the time. I drank the tea and smoked another cigaret. After a while I decided I'd go out and fasten up the gate.

So I got my robe.

The moon lighted up everything – houses and trees, poles and power lines, the whole world. I peered around the backyard before I stepped off the porch. A little breeze came along that made me close the robe.

I started for the gate.

There was a noise at the fences that separated our place from Sam Lawton's place. I took a sharp look. Sam was leaning with his arms on his fence, there being two fences to lean on. He raised his fist to his mouth and gave a dry cough.

'Evening, Nancy,' Sam Lawton said.

I said, 'Sam, you scared me.' I said, 'What are you doing up?' 'Did you hear something?' I said. 'I heard my gate unlatch.'

He said, 'I didn't hear anything. Haven't seen anything, either. It might have been the wind.'

He was chewing something. He looked at the open gate and shrugged.

His hair was silvery in the moonlight and stood up on his head. I could see his long nose, the lines in his big sad face.

I said, 'What are you doing up, Sam?' and moved closer to the fence. 'Want to see something?' he said.

'I'll come around,' I said.

I let myself out and went along the walk. It felt funny walking around outside in my nightgown and my robe. I thought to myself that I should try to remember this, walking around outside like this.

Sam was standing over by the side of his house, his pajamas way up high over his tan-and-white shoes. He was holding a flashlight in one hand and a can of something in the other.

Sam and Cliff used to be friends. Then one night they got to drinking. They had words. The next thing, Sam had built a fence and then Cliff built one too.

That was after Sam had lost Millie, gotten married again, and become a father again all in the space of no time at all. Millie had been a good friend to me up until she died. She was only forty-five when she did it. Heart failure. It hit her just as she was coming into their drive. The car kept going and went on through the back of the carport.

'Look at this,' Sam said, hitching his pajama trousers and squatting down. He pointed his light at the ground.

I looked and saw some wormy things curled on a patch of dirt.

'Slugs,' he said. 'I just gave them a dose of this,' he said, raising a can of something that looked like Ajax. 'They're taking over,' he said, and worked whatever it was that he had in his mouth. He turned his head to one side and spit what could have been tobacco. 'I have to keep at this to just come close to staying up with them.' He turned his light on a jar that was filled with the things. 'I put bait out, and then every chance I get I come out here with this stuff. Bastards are all over. A crime what they can do. Look here,' he said.

He got up. He took my arm and moved me over to his rosebushes. He showed me the little holes in the leaves.

'Slugs,' he said. 'Everywhere you look around here at night. I lay out bait and then I come out and get them,' he said. 'An awful invention, the slug. I save them up in that jar there.' He moved his light to under the rosebush.

A plane passed overhead. I imagined the people on it sitting belted in their seats, some of them reading, some of them staring down at the ground.

'Sam,' I said, 'how's everybody?'

'They're fine,' he said, and shrugged.

He chewed on whatever it was he was chewing. 'How's Clifford?' he said.

I said, 'Same as ever.'

Sam said, 'Sometimes when I'm out here after the slugs, I'll look over in your direction.' He said, 'I wish me and Cliff was friends again. Look there now,' he said, and drew a sharp breath. 'There's one there. See him? Right there where my light is.' He had the beam directed onto the dirt under the rosebush. 'Watch this,' Sam said.

I closed my arms under my breasts and bent over to where he was shining his light. The thing stopped moving and turned its head from side to side. Then Sam was over it with his can of powder, sprinkling the powder down.

'Slimy things,' he said.

The slug was twisting this way and that. Then it curled and straightened out.

Sam picked up a toy shovel, and scooped the slug into it, and dumped it out in the jar.

'I quit, you know,' Sam said. 'Had to. For a while it was getting so I didn't know up from down. We still keep it around the house, but I don't have much to do with it anymore.'

I nodded. He looked at me and he kept looking.

'I'd better get back,' I said.

'Sure,' he said. 'I'll continue with what I'm doing and then when I'm finished, I'll head in too.'

I said, 'Good night, Sam.'

He said, 'Listen.' He stopped chewing. With his tongue, he pushed whatever it was behind his lower lip. 'Tell Cliff I said hello.'

I said, 'I'll tell him you said so, Sam.'

Sam ran his hand through his silvery hair as if he was going to make it sit down once and for all, and then he used his hand to wave.

In the bedroom, I took off the robe, folded it, put it within reach. Without looking at the time, I checked to make sure the stem was out on the clock. Then I got into the bed, pulled the covers up, and closed my eyes.

It was then that I remembered I'd forgotten to latch the gate.

I opened my eyes and lay there. I gave Cliff a little shake. He cleared his throat. He swallowed. Something caught and dribbled in his chest.

I don't know. It made me think of those things that Sam Lawton was dumping powder on.

> I thought for a minute of the world outside my house, and then I
> didn't have any more thoughts except the thought that I had to
> hurry up and sleep.
>
> (Carver 1985: 204–7)

Discussion

Most noticeable in this story is how the action is predominantly 'shown'
through the use of detail and dialogue. It is left to the reader to interpret
events as the narrator takes a back seat. Initially the narrative details the
actions and mundane preoccupations of a sleepless night, leading to the
gate and the meeting with Sam. In this way it is showing the insomnia
through action. The story uses telling when the backstory is summarised:
the neighbours' relationship is given a concise history. This gives the
reader the gist of the conflict, but still leaves them wanting to know
more, and indeed imagining more. Notice also how showing isn't a
licence to overwrite or crowd the reader out with unnecessary detail. The
reader is most active in such stories; the balance of withholding and
disclosing information is crucial to this. There are many details being
offered, but there is less processed information; the reader is in charge of
the interpretation.

Dialogue and subtext

If you sit around for a while in a café or a waiting room listening to
conversations, you will notice it is fairly difficult, and often impossible,
to recall such exchanges word for word after the event. Lines of real-life
dialogue are often fragmentary; people don't finish sentences, and the
overall conversation is often without shape. Such daily conversations can
be mundane and insignificant. Yet the words will always be remembered
in your fictional exchanges, and the conversations will always be shaped
and hold a meaning, even if they are seemingly about mundane things.
You will never be presenting dialogue just for the sake of itself; it will
always have a purpose, for example illustrating things like character,
action, atmosphere, mood, and plot.

Using dialogue allows you to develop a character, as you have already
seen in Chapter 3. Once characters speak they seem to take on another
level of creation, as if they have started breathing. Dialogue can also be
useful when you have a major plot point to make. Going back to our

story of the drunken grandmother, for instance, her missing daughter might come home. If you write 'then the daughter returned', this might seem too swift for such a significant moment. If you capture the return dramatically through dialogue, you make the event more plausible. It might read like this:

As she reached for the light switch she felt a presence in the room.

A voice said, 'Hello, Mum.'

She knew the voice. 'H . . . h . . . hello . . .' she stuttered, as she looked up.

'Well, am I worth a hug?'

'A hug?' she said.

'After all these years, aren't I worth even that?'

With the above dialogue and the dialogue between the man and the woman in the park, which we looked at earlier in the chapter, there is room for the reader to climb in between the lines and invent the dynamic between each set of characters. In each dialogue the reader is presented with the challenge of constructing and interpreting the scenario and what might be happening and what is really being communicated by the characters. The words spoken in any dialogue are only part of the exchange between people; often the unspoken elements can be louder, if less articulate. As seen in Chapter 3 these unspoken words may consist of the things that the characters cannot or dare not say, or may not even know. The dialogue you give your reader must offer an indication of this other, unspoken communication, what is often referred to as the 'subtext'.

The subtext can be to do with the atmosphere between characters; implied information about the participants; and implied information about the story and plot. David Mamet says:

In the bad film, the fellow says, 'hello, Jack, I'm coming over to your home this evening because I need to get the money you borrowed from me.' In the good film, he says, 'where the hell were you yesterday?' [. . .] The less you narrate [in the dialogue], the more the audience is going to say, 'wow. What the *heck* is happening here? What the *heck* is going to happen next . . .?'

(Mamet 1992: 71)

The same is true for fiction writers trying to involve their readers. In the scene of the daughter's return, for instance, if her mother came straight out with: 'Oh, I've missed you, and I'm glad to see you, but I'm angry too. Where have you been all this time?' And if the daughter replied: 'I ran off with a boy. We had a baby together and I didn't want to tell you. Then he left me, but now I'm back. Have you got any money I could borrow?', it would be too straightforward for the reader. They would be left with nothing to imagine and the exchange would seem implausible – no one tends to talk that explicitly.

Similarly, with the exchange in the park between the man and the woman, the reader is left thinking: 'What will be okay? Why is she getting angry with him? Why is he trying to placate her? Is someone dying? Is she pregnant? What is causing the tension?' The reader is hooked. If the writer rushes into answering too many of these questions then the reader's sense of anticipation might be wasted.

Activity 7.9   Reading

Look back over the Carver story and the extracts from 'The Dying Room' and 'Hills Like White Elephants'. Identify the following elements and detail them in your notebook:

- the parts of the dialogue that seem to be masking something and getting the reader to ask questions and imagine answers;
- the parts of the dialogue that are explicit and reveal information to the reader;
- what the subtext might be about in each story.

Discussion

The sort of non-explicit dialogue that Mamet advocates is highly realistic. It attempts to imitate the unspoken exchanges between people, to use the spoken lines as a mask for what is actually being communicated. This sort of dialogue is often used in fiction writing – as you can see in the Carver story, where the dialogue covers over the cracks, barely disguising the strained atmosphere, ripe for reconciliation, between the two households. This can also be seen in the brief Hemingway extract, where the subtext is largely about the woman's doubts about the man's affection for her.

The Hammick story is different. The subtext concerns the death of the father, and the tension between mother and son resulting from this. For a large part of the story this remains below the surface of the dialogue.

In the latter half of 'The Dying Room' the dialogue becomes explicit and Hammick, explains some of the backstory, by getting the mother and son to talk about the father. The son is resistant but the mother tells him (and the reader) about his father's early years:

> It was a very comfortable, green-belt childhood. There was a cook, Inez I think, and a maid. Two maids. There was a nanny until your father went away to school. There was a big garden with a shrubbery one end to play in – though he had to play by himself most of the time, of course, being an only child. There was all that. There were also your grandparents who hated each other. They slept at different ends of the house, but in the evenings when your grandfather came home from his office they sat together in the drawing room in their own special chairs and tormented each other. Your grandmother had the edge, she was the cleverer. She was frustrated. Nowadays, I suppose, she'd have been a career woman, and perhaps not married. From all the evidence she despised men. While this ritual was going on, while they goaded and persecuted each other, your father was made to sit in a corner and play with his Meccano or read a book. He was not allowed to interrupt and he was not allowed to leave the room. At six-forty-five on the dot your grandmother would take a key from the bunch on the thin leather belt she always wore and unlock the drinks cupboard, and the serious whisky drinking – and the serious torturing – would begin.
>
> [. . .]
>
> When your father was dying I thought about the nightmare he'd had to endure while he was growing up. I wondered if it might have been responsible in some way for his illness.
>
> (Hammick 1996 [1986]: 376–377)

The implausibility of this revelation – a character being told something he should already know – is avoided by the fact that the father died when the boy was too young to remember. The mother has told him this story repeatedly, which partly explains the son's indifference. The story about the father's childhood is also motivated by the mother's irrational guilt about all the events surrounding the father's death – but especially the misgiving about her failure to cook him the sausages he requested during his final weeks. This guilt makes her repeat herself and talk randomly about the father, who, it transpires, actually died in the drawing room. This is the room that initiates the argument between mother and son, and talk of it is bound to stir painful memories.

Motivating and making such exposition plausible in this fashion is most important, as it helps conceal the fact that information is being passed to the reader. You can see that this sort of dialogue is bearing the weight of exposition in a very different way from the Carver story.

Activity 7.10 Writing

Revisit Activity 7.2. Use a character that may have been created in that exercise (the tired, loving, loathing, bored or drunken character) and write a paragraph in summary of their backstory and key elements about them (using up to 150 words). For example, with the grandmother we have already imagined a possible backstory that includes details of how she has been drinking for twenty years, is divorced, and has a daughter who mysteriously left home.

Then write a page of dialogue involving the character (using up to 200 words). Try to create a subtext, an atmosphere or some implied information for your reader, beyond what the words of the dialogue explicitly say. For examples of this sort of dialogue look back over the shown version of the grandmother's reunion with her daughter or the dialogue in the park scene.

As a final stage combine the two passages, so the backstory and dialogue are mixed (using up to 250 words). This will mean you have to make crucial decisions on what stays in and what is less relevant and should be cut. Try to drip-feed the backstory into the narrative so it doesn't all come at once.

When to show and tell

Looking at your writing in terms of showing and telling should be an ongoing task, a part of the way you conceive a story and a part of the way you edit and redraft it. This will often mean unpacking something you have summarised: you will find yourself dramatising, setting scenes, using dialogue and characters' thoughts, and asking yourself what you really meant by describing characters and events in abstract terms. You will also, from time to time, realise that you have dramatised a section that really needs passing over quickly. 'Show don't tell' is such well-used advice because first drafts tend to be laden with telling, passages that are too condensed and need unpacking. But there are occasions when 'tell don't show' is the more appropriate advice. The craft of fiction writing combines both ways of revealing information. You should be hoping to strike a happy balance in any one particular story.

References

Carver, Raymond (1985) *The Stories of Raymond Carver*, London: Picador/Pan Books.

Clarke, Lindsay (2001) 'Going the Last Inch: Some thoughts on showing and telling' in Julia Bell and Paul Magrs (eds) (2001) *The Creative Writing Coursebook*, London: Macmillan.

Dawood, N. J. (trans.) (1973) *Tales from the Thousand and One Nights*, Harmondsworth: Penguin.

Hammick, Georgina (1996 [1986]) *People for Lunch/Spoilt*, London: Vintage.

Hemingway, Ernest (1995) *The Complete Short Stories of Ernest Hemingway* London: Everyman.

James, Henry (1948) *The Art of Fiction*, London: Oxford University Press.

Joyce, James (1960 [1922]) *Ulysses*, London: Minerva.

Le Guin, Ursula K. (1998) *Steering the Craft*, Portland: The Eighth Mountain Press.

Lodge, David (1992) *The Art of Fiction*, London: Penguin.

Lubbock, Percy (1954 [1921]) *The Craft of Fiction*, London: Jonathan Cape.

Mamet, David (1992 [1991]) *On Directing Film*, London: Faber & Faber.

Mansfield, Katherine (1984) *The Stories of Katherine Mansfield*, Antony Alpers (ed.), Oxford: Oxford University Press.

O'Hagan, Andrew (2003) *Personality*, London: Faber & Faber.

Richardson, Samuel (1985 [1748]) *Clarissa*, Harmondsworth: Penguin.

8

Structure

Derek Neale

According to David Lodge the structure of any narrative should remain largely invisible – 'like the framework of girders that hold up a modern high-rise building: you can't see it, but it determines the edifice's shape and character' (Lodge 1992: 216). As Lodge goes on to say, unlike a building, a narrative's structure has more to do with time than space. This chapter will explore the notion that a narrative's structure is made up of two connected elements:

- dramatic action;
- time and its arrangement within the story.

Before we examine what dramatic action is, let's pause to consider the relationship between drama and fiction.

Author interview

Many fiction writers believe that there is a fruitful relationship between fiction and drama. Numerous novelists enjoy crossing generic boundaries by also writing scripts for dramatic media. This seems a logical outcome from Henry James' advice – that novelists should dramatise their writing. Hanif Kureishi is just such a writer. He writes for stage and screen as well as writing novels. I recorded an interview with Kureishi for The Open

University. As you read the following transcript, note some answers to the following questions:

- What does Kureishi see as the difference between writing drama and writing fiction?
- How does dialogue operate differently in drama and fiction?
- What does Kureishi say about structure?

Derek Neale (DN): The first person voice in your novel, *Intimacy* – is that similar to a stage monologue or a dramatic monologue?

Hanif Kureishi (HK): It's really just someone speaking about themselves to themselves. It's an internal monologue, really. It's a man saying to himself 'Shall I do this, shall I do that, do I feel this, do I feel that?' You could do it on the stage. It has been in fact done on the stage but it's a monologue in the sense that it is a person who's trying to work something out themselves and [the narrative voice] draws the reader into the process of their mind. It was really about – Can I write a book set during the night? It's eight o'clock at night, he's going to leave his wife in the morning. What happens during the whole of that night? So I had a structure. Like the book I'm writing now, it starts in 1975 and it ends yesterday, as it were.

DN: So structure equals time, a time span of some sort?

HK: You need some sort of container and as soon as you've found the container – it's like a football match, it's going to be 90 minutes and then whatever is going to happen will happen in between and it's rather like that. Once you've found that, then you can play in the middle of it.

DN: How does dramatic writing affect the way you write fiction?

HK: Well I write in a number of forms: movies, plays, essays, as many writers in fact have done. And every form has its constraints, and the constraints of each form are the pleasures of each form. For instance, when you are doing a movie you are working with a director and you are writing words for actors, you are also producing your creativity in front of an enormous amount of other people i.e. you're doing it with the crew. When you are writing a novel you're alone over a long period of time and quite isolated. When you are doing a play you work in a rehearsal room, quite closely with the actors and so on.

There is another sense in which they are all the same – you're telling stories and you're trying to seduce or entertain or draw your reader or audience into this world that you've created. It is really a world of characters and the dilemma is in the characters and relationships between them.

DN: Do you think in terms of scenes?

HK: Well I'm writing a novel now and what I think in terms of really is chapters. Each chapter has to move the story on, so that each one contributes something to the complete effect. You move the story forward, the characters forward and therefore the readers' interest forward each time. A novel is a dramatic form. The difference between being a writer and doing writing as therapy is that you are attempting to interest another person. If you are doing therapy you're just trying to bring about a different state of mind. If you're writing as a writer, you are very aware that this is for other people and that other people are waiting for you to have an effect on them in some way. This has to be dramatic.

DN: How does the dialogue in your stories or novels differ from the dialogue you might write for a film or a play?

HK: The dialogue in a novel probably would be more extended. When you're writing a movie you probably cut as much dialogue as you can. [In movies] we show it in pictures. With a novel the pleasure is often hearing the people speak. This would be very dramatic in the novel whereas in a movie it would tend to hold it up.

Kureishi is illuminating about the way in which writing drama differs from writing fiction, especially about how dialogue in fiction can be really important in revealing a character. He also offers some useful introductory tips about structuring your fiction – establishing a time span, for instance. His insistence that the novel form is dramatic, in the way the narrative is always pushing events forwards, echoes many definitions of dramatic action. We will now explore this further, along with other aspects of the way stories can be structured.

Dramatic action

The notion of a 'dramatic action', commonly associated with stage plays and films, has been acknowledged by fiction writers like Flannery O'Connor as a central plank of any narrative structure:

> A story is a complete dramatic action – and in good stories, the characters are shown through the action and the action is controlled through the characters, and the result of this is meaning that derives from the whole presented experience.
>
> (O'Connor 1984 [1957]: 90)

It is important to note how the word 'action' here is different from the everyday usage. 'Action' in this instance refers not to some high adventure, no gunfights or thrilling battles, but to a movement which may be just a transition in time or a change in emotional state. In Charlotte Brontë's *Jane Eyre* (1996 [1847]), for instance, the character of Jane can be seen as the embodiment of a dramatic action. She begins the novel as an orphan with a burning but ill-defined ambition; she progresses through various ordeals and situations until she comes to realising her ambition, which has to do with finding a husband but on her own terms. This movement is sweeping – ranging from youth to maturity, from innocence to experience. The story is relatively straightforward in its development. It is a process of change, witnessed by the reader – something happens and the reader sees the state of affairs before, during and after. It has:

- a beginning (Jane as orphan);
- a middle (Jane as young woman with romantic ideals which are challenged);
- an end (Jane as married woman yet independent, in terms of finance and status).

Similarly, if you consider 'The Dream', looked at in the last chapter, you will see an equally grand dramatic action. This story involves a character destitute and seeking a turn in his fortune, going on a hopeful journey, meeting with disaster then joy, eventually finding his fortune back in Baghdad, where he set off. This action is paradoxical in that it is both linear and circular – it involves the step by step pursuit of a fortune, but returns to its starting point. That is how the moral of the parable works – those seeking their fortune would do well to look closer to home.

The dramatic action is much less obvious in stories like Carver's 'I could see the smallest things'. There is no simple moral to be deduced from the action. In such a story as Carver's something happens but it isn't as large in scale as a young person growing into adulthood, or a man finding his fortune. The narrative consists of two neighbours going out in the night and talking by a gate. It begins with the narrator waking and restless; the middle is the conversation about slugs and other matters; the end is the return to bed. Yet what is the dramatic action? This is much harder to grasp, and seems to have to do with some move of reconciliation between the arguing neighbours (Sam 'used his hand to wave'), or the narrator's burgeoning realisation that her partner revolts her (his breathing at the end reminds her of the slugs Sam was trying to kill).

You can see from the Carver story that a dramatic action doesn't have to be tied in with something momentous like a death or a marriage. The main character doesn't fulfil a major goal. There doesn't have to be a fight between the characters for the conflict in the story to be apparent; the movement involved can be really quite slight and may well defy definition.

Story, plot and action

E. M. Forster famously distinguished between the way a story works and the way a plot works. For Forster a story is a 'narrative of events arranged in their time-sequence' (Forster 1976 [1927]: 87). His example:

'The king died and then the queen died.'

For Forster a plot is similar; it retains the time sequence, but with the addition of causality. So this is a plot:

'The king died and then the queen died of grief.'

Forster offers one further example:

'The queen died, no one knew why, until it was discovered that it was through grief at the death of the king.'

This, according to Forster, is a plot with mystery and therefore has great potential.

Plot is a relative element in any fiction – it can be negligible or it can be most prominent, depending on the story you wish to write. As Ursula Le Guin suggests:

> A story that has nothing but action and plot is a pretty poor affair; and some great stories have neither. To my mind, plot is merely one way of telling a story, by connecting the happenings tightly, usually through causal chains. [. . .] As for action, indeed a story must move, something must happen; but the action can be nothing more than a letter sent that doesn't arrive, a thought unspoken, the passage of a summer day. Unceasingly violent action is usually a sign that there is, in fact, no story being told.
>
> (Le Guin 1998: 117)

Whatever your regard for, or use of plot, what you need to remember is that there will always be at least two perspectives on the material you are working on:

- the whole story – the history of all the events found, imagined and researched – about which you might be writing;
- your version of the story – your eventual plotted representation of those events.

The first of these will have a certain sequential order and include all possible details. The second might have a different order and will almost certainly omit details. If you imagine the writing of a story to be like carving a figure out of wood, the 'whole story' is the lump of tree trunk that you cut from the forest, whereas 'your version' is the final shape of the carving once you've whittled away the wood you don't need.

For instance, the story might be about a woman who has reached a crisis in her life – perhaps her marriage has failed, perhaps she has always wanted to have a lot of children but her husband only ever wanted one, his precious daughter whom he idolises. Perhaps the woman is jealous of her daughter and doesn't realise it. As you can see from this rough scenario there is an enormous amount of usable conflict, material which raises structural questions. It appears to be the woman's story, so should the tale begin with the woman's birth and childhood and details of her own parents? Should it detail how the man and woman became husband and wife? These are the sorts of things that you might collect in your notebook, via your imagination and research, under the heading 'whole story'. This is the tree trunk you've cut down. But eventually you will have to choose the shape of your carving, to pick and choose which events and details you include in 'your version'.

Activity 8.1 Writing

Write a story (up to 300 words) using any or all of the details from the 'woman in crisis' scenario just described. If you find it difficult keeping within the word limit, try using one paragraph for the beginning, one for the middle and one for the end. Write in first person or third person and in whichever tense you wish, but write from one point of view, so it is one character's story. This character doesn't have to be the woman though – it can be the husband, or the daughter.

Discussion

One of the decisions you will in effect have made (possibly without realising it) concerns the dramatic action. For instance, one possible action could be how the woman comes to realise that the relationship she has with her own daughter has been shaped by the resentment she feels towards her husband. This is a version of the story that has to do with her moment of crisis and realisation, therefore details of her own childhood might seem less relevant. Such an action would start halfway through her life story and finish before the end, before her death – you wouldn't bother including details about the piano lessons she used to have at school or her first boyfriend, though you might mention how she herself was an only child and always wished for siblings.

In trying to establish 'your version' of any story you will have to make many decisions about what to include and what to leave out; be aware that in many first drafts elements from the 'whole story' get included in 'your version', elements that you may later deem to be irrelevant. This is to be expected, but something always to be watched for in editing.

Time

One of the major decisions to make when arriving at 'your version' is about where to start and where to finish – marking out the parameters of the action. In making those decisions you are dealing with one of the main building blocks of structure – time.

Time works in many different ways within a narrative. It is used to establish a present in a story, and subsequently to establish a past and the possibility of time passing and moving towards a future. This is an obvious aid in establishing movement or action, but it is also a great aid in

163

establishing what might be termed 'depth structure' – the richness of the text conveying a world which existed before the reader engaged with it and which will carry on existing after the reader leaves it. It is often this richness and depth that convinces readers that they are engaged with a believable world.

Emily Brontë's *Wuthering Heights* (1982 [1847]) begins when Lockwood, a visitor from the South, arrives at the bleak, northern farm. He is disturbed in the night by the apparition of Cathy knocking on the window, calling 'Let me in' (p. 67). He also finds the names Catherine Earnshaw, Catherine Heathcliff and Catherine Linton scratched on the window ledge (Brontë 1982 [1847]: 61) These things are obviously connected to the backstory and events that happened long before the arrival of Lockwood, who is subsequently informed of those events by Nelly, the housekeeper. In effect the novel has begun nine-tenths of the way through the story's time-frame, yet Lockwood's arrival establishes a dramatic present immediately in the mind of the reader. It is one they can identify with as fellow newcomers into this world, and other time-frames can be organised around this arrival.

Similarly, when choosing the time-scheme for a particular story, you will need to establish a dramatic present, a fulcrum around which your backstory and any forward movement can be organised. For instance, with the scenario of the 'woman in crisis', you might have the woman looking out of the window at 8.30 am, watching the younger children going to school that particular morning as your dramatic present, though the woman may regularly look out of the window in this way. The establishment of repeated 'habitual time' is easily achieved in fiction, compared to film or stage plays where the emphasis is always on the dramatic present. In fiction events can happen daily, monthly or annually; habitual behaviour can be written in a line.

You will recall from the last chapter, and the extracts from Georgina Hammick's short story 'The Dying Room', that in some stories there is a predominance of direct and reported speech. This helps establish the dramatic present of the story. In the case of 'The Dying Room' the dramatic present is situated in a kitchen during a conversation. Yet even with most of the action dramatised, as it is in Hammick's story, the habitual time elements of the story are still often related in a more telling fashion. And, as you saw in the last chapter, the narrative can benefit from an early introduction of such habitual action. 'The Dying Room' has an early summary of repeated behaviour – 'She cooks for her family [. . .].

She also supplies, on a regular basis, her local delicatessen with pâtés and terrines and tarts and quiches.' This gives backstory and a sense of a life lived through habit to the character of the mother. Not all such elements need be revealed through telling though. Something of the habit of the characters' lives and in particular the day to day relationship between mother and son in 'The Dying Room', for instance, is revealed through the characters' conversation.

Activity 8.2   Reading

Look back over 'I could see the smallest things', read in the last chapter, and the following extract from the short story 'Pigeons at Daybreak' by Anita Desai. In each identify:

- the elements that are establishing the dramatic present;
- the elements that are establishing habitual time.

> One of his worst afflictions, Mr Basu thought, was not to be able to read the newspaper himself. To have them read to him by his wife. He watched with fiercely controlled irritation that made the corners of his mouth jerk suddenly upwards and outwards, as she searched for her spectacles through the flat. By the time she found them – on the ledge above the bathing place in the bathroom, of all places: what did she want with her spectacles in *there*? – she had lost the newspaper. When she found it, it was spotted all over with grease for she had left it beside the stove on which the fish was frying. This reminded her to see to the fish before it was overdone. 'You don't want charred fish for your lunch, do you?' she shouted back when he called. He sat back then, in his tall-backed cane chair, folded his hands over his stomach and knew that if he were to open his mouth now, even a slit, it would be to let out a scream of abuse. So he kept it tightly shut.
>
> When she had finally come to the end of that round of bumbling activity, moving from stove to bucket, shelf to table, cupboard to kitchen, she came out on the balcony again, triumphantly carrying with her the newspaper as well as the spectacles. 'So,' she said, 'are you ready to listen to the news now?'
>
> 'Now,' he said, parting his lips with the sound of tearing paper, 'I'm ready.'

165

But Otima Basu never heard such sounds, such ironies or dis-
tresses. Quite pleased with all she had accomplished, and at having
half an hour in which to sit down comfortably, she settled herself
on top of a cane stool.

(Desai 1978: 98–99)

Discussion

As you can see from this extract and 'I could see the smallest things' – and
from previous stories we have looked at, such as 'The Dream' and 'The
Dying Room' – a story can be many things; it is impossible to put a
prescription on form or structure. There are common elements though.
Both the Carver and the Desai stories have a dramatic present, a 'now'.
The narratives of both establish a dramatic present fairly quickly – with
the Desai story, in the middle of a restless night; in cramped living quarters during the course of a hot, airless day (and eventually night, as the
story progresses). The dramatic present is all to do with the establishment
of time and place, and is often achieved through showing. The dramatic
present in the Desai story plots a few hours in the domestic setting of an
apartment in New Delhi. There is a power cut, meaning that Amul Basu
and his wife, Otima, have no fans. It is impossibly hot, and Amul is
asthmatic. They go to sleep on the roof but Amul doesn't know how he
will survive the night. This suggests that the story might be about a
serious health crisis, involving ambulances and possible death. However,
it is much more a story about the relationship between a husband and
wife.

Both the Carver and Desai stories contain repeated behaviour that
creates a sense of habitual time. In 'I could see the smallest things', for
instance, the habitual behaviour gets detailed in the lines of conversation, as Sam says 'I put bait out, and then every chance I get I come out
here with this stuff'. 'Pigeons at Daybreak' proceeds from lunch-time on
a certain day to dawn the next day. The story begins both with habitual
behaviour and a dramatic present. Mr Basu is seen to hate his wife reading the newspaper to him, an action in the present but one which
immediately suggests it has happened regularly before and that we are
entering a pre-existing world. In the next section of the narrative the
reader hears some of the news items that Otima Basu reads to her
husband, and how her thoughts get sidetracked as she reads. By being
given this range of news stories and thought processes, the reader is able

to see vistas of the city, to catch descriptions of climate and types of food. In effect the reader receives a detailed indication of lifestyle and living arrangements, and gets a vivid impression of the habitual elements of the Basus' existence.

Activity 8.3 Writing

Either look through your notebook and find a character that you have noted and want to work on more, or write down in your notebook a sentence about a new character.

List five habitual things about the character in your notebook. So they might go to Scotland every year to visit family; they might have a tendency to scratch their head every few minutes. But it doesn't have to be something that the character does; it could be something that is just connected to the character's life. For instance, a delivery man might call at the shop across the road from your character's house once a week or a plane might fly overhead every day at the same time.

Taking your character and the five habitual elements, write the start of a story (up to 250 words). Establish a dramatic present in which your character is situated in a particular place at a particular time, but include the five habitual elements of your character's life. Try not to clump them all together – integrate them into the other elements of your story.

Starting in the middle of the action

It is often good practice, where possible, to start stories *in medias res*, that is in the middle of the action, so the reader gets the impression they are walking in on a pre-existing world. This can, and often does, mean beginning with an exchange of dialogue. Look, for instance, at the opening of 'The Dying Room' in the last chapter, and how the conversation establishes character and place almost immediately, but also establishes the illusion that time is already in progress and events aren't just commencing for the reader's benefit. Beginning in the middle of the action can also mean simply establishing time and place. Look at this opening from another story by Hammick – 'A Few Problems in the Day Case Unit':

My name is Lettice Pomfrey and I am thirty-four years old. I am sitting in the gynaecologist's waiting room waiting to see the

> gynaecologist. I tell you this now, at the beginning, in case gynaecology is not the subject for you; in case you find some aspects of it distasteful; in case you would rather be somewhere else than in this waiting room on a hot and sunny July afternoon.
>
> (Hammick 1996 [1986]: 27)

This seems simple enough but places the reader, at a specific time and location, with a character, as well as launching an interesting rhetorical style and voice. The use of the second person pulls the reader straight into the situation, and even challenges them. Starting in the middle of the action, by this method or by using dialogue, usually means that there will be backstory to deal with later on in the narrative. You might have to tell the reader how your character got into a particular situation, for instance. Sure enough, the character-narrator, Lettice Pomfrey, soon tells the reader how many gynaecologists she has got through before arriving at this particular waiting room, though she crucially omits any further information about why she might be there.

Activity 8.4   Writing

Look back through your notebook and find another character or scenario that you want to write about. As an alternative, you can use the 'woman in crisis' scenario again, but this time write from a different point of view (i.e. if you've already used the woman, choose the husband or daughter).

Write the start of a story (up to 250 words) which launches *in medias res* – in the middle of the action. So, you might start with some dialogue, for instance, or establish a dramatic scene.

Foreshadowing

Sometimes, as well as establishing a present and a past, you will also want to leap ahead to the future, anticipating events that will happen later in the narrative. This leaping ahead is often called foreshadowing.

Stories like 'I could see the smallest things', brief narratives based primarily in a dramatic present, contain barely any foreshadowing. Stories that are mainly dramatised do not use such devices. Neither is there any obvious foreshadowing in 'The Dying Room', though this has a foreshadowing device in the title – the word 'dying' – which anticipates something to be revealed later in the narrative. By juxtaposing the phrase 'dying room' next to the opening dialogue about the 'drawing room' the reader is pulled into a time loop, wondering how the room will change, who will die or has died, and if the rooms are the same. In this way the title becomes what some might call a 'plot hook'. If the reader knows in advance that someone is going to die or has died, they become imaginatively engaged trying to work out who and how and why.

This type of foreshadowing can sometimes be straightforward, as in 'This was how Mason lost his arm.', the first sentence from 'Sawmill' a short story by Adam Thorpe (Thorpe 1998: 270), where the title and the words 'lost his arm' foreshadow the events of the story. Sometimes the foreshadowing can be more complex, as in this opening extract from *One Hundred Years of Solitude* by Gabriel García Márquez:

> Many years later, as he faced the firing squad, Colonel Aureliano Buendía was to remember that distant afternoon when his father took him to discover ice. At that time Macondo was a village of twenty adobe houses, built on the bank of a river of clear water that ran along a bed of polished stones, which were white and enormous, like prehistoric eggs. The world was so recent that many things lacked names, and in order to indicate them it was necessary to point. Every year during the month of March a family of ragged gypsies would set up their tents near the village [. . .]
>
> (García Márquez 1978 [1967]: 9)

As this is the beginning of a novel, the world being launched has many dimensions and appears in one sense fantastical (with the lack of names and the simile about the stones – 'like prehistoric eggs'). The reader is strung between some mythic time and an era when guns existed. Yet the first line about the firing squad is full of foreshadowing. It acts as a plot hook – we don't know this character yet but wonder 'How did he get into that situation? Does he die? Who is firing at him?' This incident doesn't actually occur in the narrative for another hundred pages or so, but this early glimpse leaves the reader with the anticipation of what is to come and no further detail. Notice too how, even though this is the beginning, the narrative quickly establishes habitual time, with the gypsies coming every March. This way the reader is made to feel they are looking in on a pre-existing world.

Activity 8.5   Writing

Choose one of the following:

- find another character or scenario in your notebook that you want to write about;
- use the 'woman in crisis' scenario again, but this time write from the point of view of a fourth character; for instance a marriage guidance counsellor, or a solicitor.

Write the start of the story (up to 250 words), this time beginning with a plot hook which foreshadows events that will happen in the future. So, you may like to herald an event that will be crucial to the story. The event may be momentous, like a death, but it certainly doesn't need to be. It could just be a departure, an arrival, or even a realisation. Give this story a title.

Flashback and repetition

The art of storytelling consists largely of knowing where to leave holes for readers to climb into the narrative. Time shifts and loops are part of that process and an important way of structuring your story. Your handling of time can give the narrative a real sense of depth. The dramatic present acts as a stabilising force, from where the movement of a narrative is worked out, and from where the narrative can flit backwards and forwards in time so as to push the action towards its fulfilment.

However, the present of a story can be too fast or too dominant. Without temporal variation the pace of a story can seem unrelenting. Look back at 'The Dream', specifically at the plot and how events are sequenced. You will recall that events in this story proceed in a straight-forward, linear fashion, from one point to the next, at a rapid pace. There doesn't appear to be any backstory or foreshadowing.

Stories vary in the amount they adhere to the forward drive of the dramatic present. The form and style in *One Hundred Years of Solitude* are such that the dramatic present is sometimes fractured both by forward leaps in time (as with the firing squad) and also by leaps backward. These latter, retrospective leaps towards dramatic moments in the backstory are termed 'flashbacks', and are often associated with a character's or narrator's memory. Some narratives rely more heavily than others on this technique.

For instance, Toni Morrison's *Beloved* (1988 [1987]) is structured around flashbacks. Ostensibly set in Ohio in 1873 after the abolition of slavery, the novel is about Sethe, a former slave who killed one of her children so the child wouldn't become a slave. The child comes back to haunt the house where Sethe lives and acts as a catalyst for all the characters' stories from the time before abolition. In this way the past is seen to haunt the present and, in terms of form, the dramatic present of Morrison's narrative is constantly ruptured by flashbacks of characters and episodes from a time prior to 1873.

Activity 8.6   Reading

Reread 'Girl' by Jamaica Kincaid, which you looked at in Chapter 6. In your notebook write down how it is structured and how time is working within the story. Take particular note of how repetition is used.

Discussion

Some stories don't work in a straightforward progression or even have a dramatic present. 'Girl' seems to work on the basis of repetition. Habitual time and the creation of a world take precedence over the establishment of a specific time or location, or the movement through a dramatic episode. Certain elements are repeated at regular intervals – like 'benna' and 'Sunday'. Certain clauses and syntactical formations are also repeated so that, combined with the use of the second person, the story sounds incantatory. Variations in the repetitions and voice, such as the last line about touching the bread, are then most noticeable. They act as structural markers, as do the lines about 'becoming a slut', a strand which finds its culmination in this final line: 'you mean to say that after all you are really going to be the kind of woman who the baker won't let near the bread?' The narrative is ostensibly cyclical in form, though some might say that this final shift, coupled to the hint of rebellion in some of the 'answering back', constitutes a dramatic action.

Repetition can also be used in a less radical fashion. For instance, in 'The Dying Room', notice how the 'wireless' features at the start of the story. It also features in the middle of the narrative, as the argument between mother and son reaches a new pitch and the son calls on a witness to back him up:

171

Martin found you frightening, he said. D'you remember Martin?

That's okay, I found Martin frightening, his mother said.

When I say 'frightening' I mean 'posh', he said. I met Martin in the pub the other night and he seemed a bit down and fed up with life – well, with his job really – and I asked him if he'd like to get away to the country this weekend. He wanted to know if you were going to be there. I said probably you would, it was your house. And he said, Well, think I'll give it a miss then. No offence, but your mother and her 'drawing rooms' and 'wirelesses' and 'gramophones' are a bit posh for me. He pronounced it 'poshe'.

(Hammick 1996: 375)

Then the word 'wireless' features again right at the end of the story, when the mother and son have reached a point of emotional resolution. This is the son speaking and then the mother responding:

Look, I'd better go and get Grandpa, I'd better go and find the girls.

Could you bring me my wireless at the same time? his mother said, I want to hear the news. I'm not sure where I left it, downstairs I think, in the – in some room or other.

(Hammick 1996: 380)

You can see that the rephrasing of the opening line of the story ('I think I left my wireless in the drawing room, his mother said. Could you get it? I'd be grateful.') creates a note of structural resolution. The repeated word 'wireless' acts like a marker for the beginning, middle and end of the story. Repetition of certain features in this way can be used as a deeper structural device to reinforce the action. If you recall, one of the suggested possibilities for the 'woman in crisis' scenario was that she herself was an only child and had wished for siblings when young. This echo could, in effect, act as structural reinforcement for the main action of the story. Habitual elements are also structurally useful in this respect. Stories can be built using the scaffolding of the daily plane flying overhead, or the annual trip to Scotland, or the weekly work routine.

In both the Carver story and the Desai extract repetition can be seen to point up the main action and structure. In 'I could see the smallest things', Cliff's breathing is mentioned in the opening passage ('awful to listen to'), and then again at the end ('He cleared his throat'). The slugs appear in the middle of the story, in the conversation with Sam, and again at the end when Cliff's breathing difficulty and dribbling remind Nancy of the slugs. Sometimes the repetition can be the return of the exact same element; sometimes it can just consist of an echo, the appearance of something similar but not quite the same. In 'Pigeons at Daybreak' affliction is a structural and thematic element, which is repeated in different guises throughout the narrative – we get it in the first line about the newspaper reading, and then later on in the story in reference to Basu's chronic asthma. Crucially the omniscient point of view reveals both main characters at various times to be afflicted, though Otima is less liable to use that word.

Activity 8.7   Writing

Look through your notebook for characters or a location that you might want to develop (instead, if you need it, use 'tent' or 'pier' or 'hairdresser' as a prompt).

Then, again in your notebook, write a 'paragraph story' (up to 100 words) containing an element that is repeated at least once, and another element that is repeated with variation. For example:

> She stood on the bridge with her unfastened jacket billowing like a sail in the wind. In the distance she saw the island with its lighthouse and white cottages, and speculated about how long the ferry would take to cross the rough channel. He came up to her and said he wanted to go home. 'Why?' she asked, but he didn't answer, clinging with his gloved hands to the rails, buffeted by the swirling gusts. She took off her jacket and wrapped it around him, before leading him back towards the red brick houses on the quay.

Here the jacket is repeated and the housing varies – from being 'white cottages' on the island to 'red brick houses' on the quay.

Discussion

You can see from the example that even in such a brief narrative, the paragraph appears to be a story because events are situated in time, and there is a beginning, middle and end. Repeated or echoed elements and motifs appeal to the reader's associative memory, allowing them to make more lateral connections. If used lightly, these can be fruitful devices that reinforce a structure, complementing the more logical and linear progression of a narrative. As with most devices though, if over-used the echoes might seem implausible and clumsy, the writing can seem too planned or schematised. The craft lies in using such tactics judiciously.

Activity 8.8   Writing

Bearing in mind that you are trying to write a story with an element of repetition, pick a scenario from your notebook that you want to develop, or alternatively develop one of the following ideas:

- an event repeated with the same or different participants – two dinner parties, for instance;
- a repeated event which when repeated is on a different scale – a birthday spent alone and one spent with a group of friends, for instance;
- a character who echoes another character – for instance, a teacher loath to admit he doesn't know something, echoed in a boy who won't admit he did wrong;
- a location which is echoed – for example, the old people's home where a character is resident echoing the hotel where she worked as a girl.

Now write a story (up to 1000 words) which, as well as using repetition, also shows some or all of these technical elements:

- a dramatic present;
- a dramatic action;
- habitual time;
- flashback;
- foreshadowing;
- starting *in medias res*.

Because this story is longer than the paragraph story, the repetitions and echoes might be larger in scale.

Bringing the parts together

The structure of any narrative is arrived at through the organisation of time, from choosing where and how the narrative should start, to deciding upon the dramatic present. As a writer you have to sift through the 'whole story' in order to decide upon 'your version' – where you are going to end up, and the arrangement of the various components. In doing this you establish a dramatic action, a movement – things were one way, now they're different, however slightly, but something happens and you will have shown the transition. You may also use the device of repetition to help reinforce this movement and organisation of time. It is through these various techniques that your narrative will gain a sense of depth.

You don't necessarily need any or all of these elements in place before you start writing. Structural organisation is often arrived at during the writing. Eventually it will be the stability of your structure that reassures the reader. It is also the structure which invites the reader to be imaginatively active within a story. Those are the primary functions of your structure – getting your reader to trust you and then getting them to do some work.

References

Brontë, Charlotte (1996 [1847]) *Jane Eyre*, Harmondsworth: Penguin.

Brontë, Emily (1982 [1847]) *Wuthering Heights*, Harmondsworth: Penguin.

Carver, Raymond (1985) *The Stories of Raymond Carver*, London: Picador/Pan Books.

Desai, Anita (1978) *Games at Twilight and Other Stories*, London: Penguin.

Forster, E.M. (ed.) (1976 [1927]) *Aspects of the Novel*, Harmondsworth: Pelican/Penguin.

García Márquez, Gabriel (1978 [1967]) *One Hundred Years of Solitude*, Gregory Rabassa (tr.), London: Picador.

Hammick, Georgina (1996 [1986]) *People for Lunch/Spoilt*, London: Vintage.

Hind, Angela (producer) (2005) interview, A215 *Creative Writing* CDI, 'Writing Fiction', Milton Keynes: The Open University/Pier Productions.

Kincaid, Jamaica (1983) *At the Bottom of the River*, New York: Farrar Straus & Giroux.

Le Guin, Ursula K. (1998) *Steering the Craft*, Portland: The Eighth Mountain Press.

Lodge, David (1992) *The Art of Fiction*, London: Penguin.

Morrison, Toni (1988 [1987]) *Beloved*, London: Picador.

O'Connor, Flannery (1984 [1957]) *Mystery and Manners*, New York Farrar, Straus & Giroux.

Thorpe, Adam (1998) 'Sawmill' in Carmen Callil and Craig Raine (eds) *New Writing 7*, London: Vintage.

9

The story and the reader

Derek Neale

From these chapters on fiction writing it is possible to accumulate a list of elements that might, or even should, be included in any story that you write. A story should:

- have at least one character;
- be set somewhere;
- be written from a certain point of view;
- have a structure organised in time;
- have a balance between showing and telling in the way it is revealed to its reader.

Yet still there is a sense that something is missing, and that any list of ingredients will never be enough. Stories are more than this. There are no prescriptions for a story's content, for instance, as you can see from the stories we've looked at in previous chapters, and no doubt have also seen in your other reading. A story can be about anything. Stories can also take many forms and while they have to give the reader the impression that this 'anything' is unique and worthy of their attention, the narrative has to be fashioned in a recognisable and comprehensible way. Let's hear a writer's testimony about how he approaches his work – and what he thinks are the most important parts of a fiction.

Author interview

The following interview with the novelist Andrew Cowan was recorded for an Open University course. Cowan's novels are distinguished by a meticulous attention to detail and a highly realistic range of characters and events. I asked him about his novels *Pig*, *Common Ground* and *Crustaceans*, and in particular how he achieves his particular brand of realism. While reading this transcript of the interview, ask these questions:

- What does Cowan say about the evolution of his stories?
- How are the stories connected to his own life?
- How does he plan his novels?
- How does he structure time?
- How does he perceive his reader?

Andrew Cowan (AC): Each of my books is different. *Pig* is the miraculous one and it came to me entire. It just arrived. The beginning of the story, the middle and the end were all there from the very beginning.

Derek Neale (DN): Well that raises the question – if it was known already, how did it interest you as you were writing it?

AC: I say it's known; it's a glimmer. If I actually knew it entire there would be absolutely no reason to put it down on paper. I think every writer writes in order to find out what it is they're trying to say. Every book is a kind of journey of exploration where you are looking for the words which will give form to the glimmer. I've done more and more research as I've gone on. With *Pig* I was a little bit blithe and I just set off to tell the story. It was going to be about a pig and I'd never met a pig, I didn't know the first thing about pigs. So, I took a book out of the library and read it and I accumulated one sheet of A4 of useful information about pigs, such as it takes exactly three months, three weeks and three days for a sow to produce the piglets and that a boar's tackle is corkscrew-shaped. These kinds of things were interesting so I wrote those down but I also drew on my memories of having dogs when I was a child. So the pig in *Pig* is really a description of my collie dogs when I was a boy.

At one point I did realise I knew nothing about the boiling of swill or the regulations concerning that and I wrote to the Strathclyde veterinary authority to ask them if it was illegal to boil swill or not. I was living in a third floor tenement flat in the heart of Govan in Glasgow. They sent out the inspectors early in the morning because they thought I was a pig rustler. A certain number of pigs had gone missing in Renfrewshire and they suspected I must be keeping them in my tenement flat. But I did find out from that experience how you boil pig swill.

I had the idea for *Pig*, I thought I knew what the story was, beginning to end; actually finding the words was desperately hard and it took six years to write and it was stop-start. I would lose interest, go away and come back to it. I also found other ways to make the tedium, the difficulty, the familiarity bearable and one of those strategies was to write very long letters to friends. Another one was to keep journals, recording things I could see from my front window (I was living in Glasgow at the time, in a very rough neighbourhood); things that were happening in the school where I worked at the time – it was my first proper job, everything was new to me, therefore interesting, so I was recording that. My partner was pregnant so I was recording the journey through to childbirth and beyond. The first year of my daughter's life was all recorded in a journal. So I was actually writing journals in preference to writing *Pig* and I was writing long letters to a friend in preference to writing *Pig*.

When *Pig* was finished I had this idea of putting together those journals, the journey towards a birth and those letters which were mostly written to a friend who was on a journey round the globe. At the same time I was keeping newspaper clippings, thinking: 'Oh that might make a good story; that might make a good piece of material to feed into a novel.' When *Pig* was finished I found I'd collected an awful lot of material about New Age travellers and their protest against the building of roads through protected sites, protected woodlands and the like, so that became part of the story of *Common Ground*. I have a common which is being fought over by developers on the one hand and these New Age types on the other, amongst the New Age types is a couple who are making a journey towards the birth; so all these things fed in.

DN: Interestingly the way you describe the writing of *Pig*, it is like a process of procrastination or putting off. You're writing other things instead of writing what you are supposed to be writing.

AC: With *Pig* there was an awful lot of work avoidance, an awful lot of nest circling, but that's become my habit, that's my way of working. I can't settle down to work until I've first of all cleared every other possible distraction out of the way. So, ironing, washing up, taking the dog for a walk, shopping, all these things are higher priorities to me than writing because I can't possibly write if they're nagging at me. I think the nest circling is a necessary part of the process. You're doing it for a reason and if you feel this desperate urgency not to write but to go shopping, it's probably because the story, your unconscious, whatever it is which is going to produce this story, needs time. It needs to gestate; it needs to cook at the back of your mind. All this moving around is actually productive and fruitful. It's not time wasting. I am an advocate of staring out of the window; I think you should.

DN: The method in *Pig* seems to be concerned with writing about domestic details: drinking tea, smoking cigarettes. How did you arrive at this method?

AC: I think it's there in all of my books. I do notice things. It's how I get from one point of the narrative to another point. What I know is that I need two sentences to get me from this point to that point. What are those two sentences going to say? Well often they are just going to tell us what the room looks like or a character is going to chase a tea bag around a teacup. It is just a way of making a bridge between narrative moments. I build up a narrative by noticing.

In my last novel I have actually tried to use this in my central character, a humdrum private detective. It is his job to notice things. The trouble is he notices things which aren't of consequence. What he is not noticing is what's going wrong in his own domestic life, in his marriage and also in his own interior. He doesn't know himself. And so this obsessive noticing of detail has an ironical function in the novel.

DN: Did you plan *Pig* or did you plan *Crustaceans* or *Common Ground*?

AC: I think in scenes; I build a narrative by scenes. I think that's what I do. I write passages. Each passage is a scene. And then I move on to the next scene. And I build a narrative like this in coherent scenes, each with a beginning, middle and an end. And they should cover over that particular passage of time so that the reader feels securely located. If you create a scene it's a bit like you create a room and the reader can enter it, imaginatively sit down, relax, take in what's going on. I don't tend to plot things in advance. I never draw a diagram of how my book's going to go. My method is to begin with the very first sentence. I write the first sentence and then I re-write it. And re-write it obsessively until I feel happy with it. And then I write the second sentence. When I have, say, five or six or seven sentences I have a paragraph, let's say, I will read through the whole thing for rhythm and then I will go back and start revising the first sentence so that the whole thing flows. I always write to a particular cadence in my head and if it doesn't sound like me, then I feel very uneasy and unable to continue.

DN: How do you go about organising time in this way that you work, sentence by sentence?

AC: In the case of *Pig* there is quite a clever beginning but it's only clever in retrospect. So I begin with the grandmother's death. Grandad wakes, Grandma's dead. The pig is squealing in the garden. The boy narrates all of this as if he was there, which of course he couldn't have been. The implication is that the grandfather subsequently must have told him it as a story. I just set off like that and it kind of works, so I went with it. I think now I wouldn't allow myself to do that. I would say no, you have to be more logical in this. It does then proceed fairly chronologically. It takes place over the course of one summer. It's fairly uncomplicated. *Common Ground* has a pre-given structure because the two characters, they find they are going to have a baby. So the first seven chapters are monthly accounts of the development of the child. With *Crustaceans* there is a very complex structure. Here, there is a man who is driving out to the East Anglian coast on the 22nd December in the imaginary company of his son, who died six months earlier. By reconstructing his life in narrative, the father is trying to bring him back to life.

The father, the narrator, starts to remember things about his own childhood. There's first of all the narrative which occurs on the day. That's the spine of the book. We keep coming back to the 22nd December, in the present tense. Then there's this other narrative which begins with the boy and describes his growth from birth to the age of six when he dies. Then there's another narrative, which goes right back to the father's childhood and recounts in chronological order, his growth as a child into maturity. There is then another narrative, which is the father meeting the boy's mother at Art School, twelve years previously. That narrative describes their marriage. So there are four narratives going on in this book.

I did actually keep a kind of chart but it wasn't a chart to plan where I was going. It was a chart to map where I'd been. Each time I finished a chapter I would précis it, a short paragraph. I would write in the chapter number, the number of words in the chapter, the time when the events of this chapter occurred, and then the first line, to remind me how it begins, then three or four or five lines of plot description and then the last line so I'd know how it signs off. Written up on sheets of A4 and they were pinned to a pin board in front of me as I wrote. So I could always look up and see where I've been. The reason I did it was because there is a balancing act going on. It's a bit like building a piece of sculpture. You want all the bits to be in harmony and in proportion. I had to keep looking at it to see whether perhaps I had too much of the child's story or perhaps there was too much of the narrator's own childhood. Perhaps it was becoming very heavy in that strand. And that strand is tilting the balance of the narrative. So I'd keep looking at what I'd done so far, thinking, well, maybe this next chapter should be about the parent's marriage to balance out the other strands.

DN: How and when do you use dialogue in your stories? What do you think it adds to the storytelling?

AC: I think I put dialogue in partly as a kind of punctuation. As you are writing you feel this might be becoming a little bit tedious. And by putting in dialogue it's a bit like putting a comma in a sentence. It just gives you pause for breath. I put in a bit of dialogue and I feel like the text breathes. Another reason is that the characters are allowed to reveal themselves to each other rather than the narrator having to tell the reader about the characters. So I give the characters voices. They're allowed to interact with each other. And the reader is allowed to hear what they are saying and get to know them that way rather than have me tell them what to think about the characters. Another thing I think that dialogue does, it gives the characters a chance to test each other out – they can test, they can probe each other.

I used to be an oral historian. I used to tape record interviews with elderly people and transcribe them. The transcripts are all "ums" and "aahs" and *non sequiturs* and sentences, which drift off and lose their memory. If you were to truly represent the way that people actually speak, you'd end up with a complete mess on the page. When you write dialogue you are constructing something very artificial indeed.

There are three chapters in *Pig* where the narrator, the boy Danny, goes to visit his grandfather. Those three chapters were the easiest pieces of writing I've ever done because that is my grandfather's voice. And it came to me as if he was speaking directly to me which is a wonderful thing – although he never said any of those things, he never kept pigs; he didn't know any of those things. I just put those words into his mouth. But he's speaking them directly to me. I found those three chapters a pleasure to write. They were actually over too quickly.

You can see that in talking about his own writing process, Cowan talks here about many of the topics we have explored throughout the book – from using your own experience in your writing, through showing the story via detail and dialogue, to structuring a story using time. Cowan's method of writing the story in scenes is particularly interesting, as is his accompanying consideration for the reader – making each scene like an inviting room into which the reader can enter and start imagining. Note here how much emphasis and consideration Cowan gives to his reader.

Cowan writes a particular brand of fiction. Each writer will have his or her own style and method. Each will offer a different kind of testimony. Yet it is particularly fascinating to hear Cowan testify to the personal source of the events, characters – and sometimes even animals – in his fictions. As it is equally reassuring to note that he seems often to be voyaging into the dark, knowing where he is going but not fully able to see. That mix of blindness, optimism and determination will be essential when writing your own stories.

Activity 9.1 Reading

Read over all the pieces of fiction you have produced so far. Try to identify:

- the ones which you consider to be complete stories and why;
- the ones you consider to be part of much bigger stories and why.

Discussion

Some stories will seem complete even though they are comparatively brief; some will appear to demand a novel-length narrative because of the content or theme. Some stories will be incomplete not because of their length but because some element or other just doesn't sit well with the other elements. On occasions you might be able to identify the element straightaway. Sometimes it will take a lot of editing before you realise that you have the order wrong, for instance, or that you've given too much prominence to a particular scene or character. The opinion of other readers is valuable in these instances, but in the end you're the final arbiter of a story's finishing point.

Long or short stories

One of the biggest decisions to be made about a piece of fiction is how long it should be. Often this decision seems to be made by what you are writing about. As Irish writer Frank O'Connor says: 'There is simply no criterion of the length of a short story other than that provided by the material itself' (O'Connor 1963 [1962]: 27). The same could be said of longer narratives. For instance, you might imagine a scene – with two people sitting on the shores of a lake. You might be able to picture immediately why the characters come to the lake every year, why the surrounding landscape has significance for these characters, and you might start picturing some moments in those preceding years, see some other characters and some of the causality surrounding events. Just from one scene you might find that you are getting involved in a web of connected elements that can't be contained in 1000, 5000 or 10,000 words: it would seem to demand a novel-length narrative.

Equally possible, you might picture the scene by the lake and not want or be able to do anything more with it. You won't want to develop the characters and take them to another location, to another moment in time and a wider fictional world. Some ideas have to be left small, though their effect isn't necessarily small. They are snapshots, captured moments in time that would lose something if they were elaborated upon.

The briefer short stories are sometimes called 'sudden' fictions. These are usually under 2000 words long, and might include some of the stories you've considered in these chapters – those by Kincaid and Carver.

184

Such narratives can be as brief as a paragraph long; they can read like poems or overheard conversations or anecdotes, as much as stories. The extreme of this is the one-sentence story, such as the following from Linh Dinh:

> 'Travel books fascinated him so much that he spent his entire life chained to his desk, with the curtains drawn, reading them.'
>
> (Dinh 2004: 41)

There are extremely brief stories which use dialogue, as in 'MA' by Leonard Michaels:

> 'I said, "Ma, do you know what happened?" She said, "Oh, my God."'
>
> (Michaels 1975: 36)

Some might say that these are not actually stories, yet they have the structure of beginning, middle and end – in 'MA', for instance, the middle is very much left to the reader's imagination. More often sudden fictions are a little longer than these, allowing for more detail about character and setting and more development of the dramatic action. From the two alternative versions of the lake scenario, mentioned above, you might assume that there is a direct correlation between the passage of time within a story and the story's narrative length. This is not so. The decision about length of story isn't just about gauging narrative time; it is also connected to a decision about form and technique.

For instance, consider two stories you've already read: 'I could see the smallest things' and 'The Dream'. As we've seen Carver's story is focused on a dramatic scene at a garden gate, a moment in time which is realised through a balance of showing and telling, though there is a predominance of the former. Its brevity matches the duration of time within it. 'The Dream', by contrast, moves over a considerable period of time, yet it is also a brief narrative. The form – telling the story as a form of parable – defines the length. James Joyce's *Ulysses* (1960 [1922]) covers the events of just one day but the extensively detailed narrative runs to almost 1000 pages. Two of the stories we have considered – 'Pigeons at Daybreak' and 'The Dying Room' – run for several thousand words even though they are based on relatively short periods of time. They aren't quite as momentary as 'I could see the smallest things', but are considerably longer in terms of pages. The length of a story is dependent not just on content and the duration of events, but also on your individual approach to those elements. The form you choose reflects your intention as a writer and your attitude to what you are writing about. To illustrate this, let's consider a little more of 'Pigeons at Daybreak', the start of which you looked at in the last chapter. The story comes to an end when Otima discovers that the electricity has come back on and, pleased and relieved, rushes to tell her husband who is still on the roof of their apartment block:

> She bustled up the stairs. I'll bring him down – he'll get some hours of sleep after all, she told herself.
>
> 'It's all right,' she called out as she went up to the terrace again. 'The electricity is on again. Come, I'll help you down – you'll get some sleep in your own bed after all.'
>
> 'Leave me alone,' he replied, quite gently.
>
> 'Why? Why?' she cried. 'I'll help you. You can get into your own bed, you'll be quite comfortable—'
>
> 'Leave me alone,' he said again in that still voice. 'It is cool now.'
>
> It was. Morning had stirred up some breeze off the sluggish river Jumna beneath the city walls, and it was carried over the rooftops of the stifled city, pale and fresh and delicate. It brought with it the morning light, as delicate and sweet as the breeze itself, a pure pallor unlike the livid glow of artificial lights. This lifted higher and higher into the dome of the sky, diluting the darkness there till it, too, grew pale and gradually shades of blue and mauve tinted it lightly.
>
> The old man lay flat and still, gazing up, his mouth hanging open as if to let it pour into him, as cool and fresh as water.
>
> Then, with a swirl and flutter of feathers, a flock of pigeons hurtled upwards and spread out against the dome of the sky – opalescent, sunlit, like small pearls. They caught the light as they rose, turned brighter till they turned at last into crystals, into prisms of light. Then they disappeared into the soft, deep blue of the morning.
>
> (Desai 1978: 106–107)

The fact that Desai's story ends at dawn, not dusk, and with the beautiful image of the pigeons, 'like small pearls', transcending the city, rather than something bleaker, brings a note of hope to what might otherwise be seen as a claustrophobic tale.

Elizabeth Bowen writes:

> As to each new story, once it has been embarked on, a number of decisions have to be made – as to the size (or length), as to treatment (or manner of handling) and, most of all, as to what is this particular story's aim? What is, or should be, this particular story's scope? What is this particular story really about, and how best can what it *is* about be shown? To an extent, such decisions are made instinctively, but intellectual judgment must come in also. [. . .] Each new story (if it is of any value) will make a whole fresh set of demands: no preceding story can be of any help.

(Bowen 1965: 8)

By asking these sorts of questions of your stories – especially 'What is the story really about?' and 'How best can this be shown?' – you will be more able to recognise when you have a novel on your hands, a sudden fiction, or something in between.

Activity 9.2   Reading

Read the following edited extract from 'Writing Short Stories' by the American writer Flannery O'Connor, an essay where she talks about her own stories and comments on how would-be writers might go about writing short stories. In your notebook reflect on what O'Connor suggests might be the important elements of a short story.

> A story is a complete dramatic action — and in good stories, the characters are shown through the action and the action is controlled through the characters, and the result of this is meaning that derives from the whole presented experience. [. . .]
>
> Fiction operates through the senses, and I think one reason that people find it so difficult to write stories is that they forget how much time and patience is required to convince through the senses. No reader who doesn't actually experience, who isn't made to feel, the story is going to believe anything the fiction writer merely tells him. The first and most obvious characteristic of fiction is that

it deals with reality through what can be seen, heard, smelt, tasted, and touched.

Now this is something that can't be learned only in the head; it has to be learned in the habits. It has to become a way that you habitually look at things. [. . .]

Fiction writers who are not concerned with these concrete details are guilty of what Henry James called 'weak specification.' The eye will glide over their words while the attention goes to sleep. [. . .]

However, to say that fiction proceeds by the use of detail does not mean the simple, mechanical piling-up of detail. Detail has to be controlled by some overall purpose, and every detail has to be put to work for you. Art is selective. What is there is essential and creates movement [. . .] and there has to be a beginning, a middle, and an end, though not necessarily in that order. [. . .]

Meaning is what keeps the short story from being short. I prefer to talk about the meaning in a story rather than the theme of a story. People talk about the theme of a story as if the theme were like the string that a sack of chicken feed is tied with. They think that if you can pick out the theme, the way you pick the right thread in the chicken-feed sack, you can rip the story open and feed the chickens. But this is not the way meaning works in fiction.

When you can state the theme of a story, when you can separate it from the story itself, then you can be sure the story is not a very good one. The meaning of a story has to be embodied in it, has to be made concrete in it. A story is a way to say something that can't be said any other way, and it takes every word in the story to say what the meaning is. [. . .]

The peculiar problem of the short-story writer is how to make the action he describes reveal as much of the mystery of existence as possible. He has only a short space to do it in and he can't do it by statement. He has to do it by showing, not by saying, and by showing the concrete—so that his problem is really how to make the concrete work double time for him.

In good fiction, certain of the details will tend to accumulate meaning from the action of the story itself, and when this happens they become symbolic in the way they work. [. . .]

There are two qualities that make fiction. One is the sense of mystery and the other is the sense of manners. You get the manners from the texture of existence that surrounds you. In most good stories it is the character's personality that creates the [mystery and] action of the story. [. . .]

If you start with a real personality, a real character, then something is bound to happen; and you don't have to know what before you begin. In fact it may be better if you don't know what before you begin. You ought to be able to discover something from your stories. If you don't, probably nobody else will.

(O'Connor 1984: 90–106)

Discussion

For O'Connor the short story is about people – characters who are realised through dramatic action and through the senses. Stories deal in what 'can be seen, heard, smelt, tasted, and touched'. This is a useful reminder. The writer learns the habit of observing the world in this way, rather than trying to write in an abstract fashion; the writer learns to 'show' things rather than say them. The sort of detail that is shown should always have a purpose; it should always be central to the action of the story and is never there just for its own sake.

O'Connor suggests stories are made of two important qualities: 'the sense of mystery and [. . .] the sense of manners'. The latter means the imitation of something from real life – the way people behave and speak, for instance. This was explored in Chapters 3 and 4 on character and setting. 'Mystery' resembles Forster's notion of the plot with the most potential, the one that contains an unknown element (explored in the last chapter). It is also very much connected to character – as O'Connor says – 'a story always involves, in a dramatic way, the mystery of personality.' Mystery in its more conventional sense ('Why did it happen?') and suspense ('What might happen?') are certainly desirable qualities to have in any story, but should be there for a purpose. O'Connor talks about mystery in different contexts – the 'mystery of personality' as you have just seen but also 'the mystery of existence'. These all add a richer connotation to the term than the usual 'who-done-it' meaning. You might like to survey all the stories we have looked at so far and try to identify what the element of mystery might be.

Elsewhere in the essay O'Connor suggests form and structure are organic elements that evolve together with the content of a story – quite the opposite of how we might picture them (and how others have depicted them: remember Lodge's 'girders', for instance).

Endings and your reader

If you imagine a story about a funeral, the mystery could consist of a stranger attending the wake; it could consist of an unknown cause of death; or it could simply be a character not really knowing how they felt about the dead person. The mystery could be any number of things. Keeping something unknown is an important dynamic in any story. If everything is too obviously and too readily revealed to your reader, then the story is less likely to work. Your reader will need to be asking 'how' or 'why' at any one point in the narrative, in however small a fashion, and often they will be asking both questions simultaneously.

In each story you write your reader will go on a journey and will end up in a place which is both expected and surprising. The reader will be following every little crumb that you drop on the trail, asking and attempting to answer questions as they proceed. As Elizabeth Bowen suggests:

> Story involves action. Action towards an end not to be foreseen (by the reader) but also towards an end which, having *been* reached, must be seen to have been from the start inevitable.
> (Bowen 1948, quoted in Allen 1958: 178)

In some narratives the uniting of expectation and surprise may not be easy, and a straightforward dramatic resolution might not be viable. For instance, the conventional endings for comedy (a marriage) and tragedy (a death) are often not suitable or even possible. Consider 'Pigeons at Daybreak', for instance, where the ending is one which finds the electricity supply restored and the light rising on a new day. Neither of the main characters dies or deserts the scene. There is an emotional shift, full of pathos, but one which is also strangely intangible. The mystery of their relationship isn't explained. In many ways Otima and Amul Basu at the end are still perplexed within the predicament of their lives; the conflict doesn't reach a point of closure.

Each story you write will pursue its mystery in its own fashion. This doesn't mean it will be fully explained by the end. Often this would be undesirable. Charles Baxter says that one of the strengths of sudden fiction is that it can end 'with a suggestion – a play of light – rather than an explicit insight' (Baxter 1989: 25). Closure in longer narratives might also be unrealistic and impossible to achieve. *Jane Eyre* provides a model of complete closure when Charlotte Brontë begins the concluding chapter with Jane's statement 'Reader, I married him' (Brontë 1996 [1847]: 498). This is the culmination of the romantic quest, but novels aren't always resolved so conclusively. The modern sensibility often demands an emotionally realistic and, therefore, possibly more complex resolution. For instance, Tim Winton's novel *The Riders* (1995 [1994]) contains a central quest to find the protagonist's missing wife and to discover the reasons for her disappearance. The novel doesn't provide any satisfactory answers to this quest; by the end the protagonist has reached an emotional acceptance of his newly defined life but has not found his wife or fully explained her absence.

To plan or not to plan

Flannery O'Connor wrote a short story called 'Good Country People', which she talks about in the rest of her essay, 'Writing Short Stories'. In this story a woman with a PhD has a wooden leg, and becomes smitten by a Bible salesman who eventually steals her false limb. O'Connor admits that when paraphrased like this the story sounds like a bad joke. Yet the action of the story makes the individual elements and events of the narrative work in much more than a literal and simply comic fashion. Some elements within the story start to take on symbolic significance. For instance, the stolen leg finally reveals the woman's emotional affliction. Flannery O'Connor describes the evolution of her story in the following way:

> I wouldn't want you to think that in that story I sat down and said, 'I am now going to write a story about a Ph.D. with a wooden leg, using the wooden leg as a symbol for another kind of affliction.' I doubt myself if many writers know what they are going to do when they start out. When I started writing that story, I didn't know there was going to be a Ph.D. with a wooden leg in it. I merely found myself one morning writing a description of two women that I knew something about, and before I realized it, I had equipped one of them with a daughter with a wooden leg. As the story progressed, I brought in the Bible salesman, but I had no idea

what I was going to do with him. I didn't know he was going to steal that wooden leg until ten or twelve lines before he did it, but when I found out that this was what was going to happen, I realized that it was inevitable. This is a story that produces a shock for the reader, and I think one reason for this is that it produced a shock for the writer.

(O'Connor 1984: 100)

O'Connor speaks as though the writing just happened that way as she thought of the content. She also emphasises the need for the writer to experience some sense of revelation or shock, and how this transmits something essential to the reader. Similarly Elizabeth Bowen says: 'The novelist's perception of his characters takes place *in the course of the actual writing of the novel*' (Bowen 1948, quoted in Allen 1958: 179). When writing novels Louis de Bernières (2004) says that he sees the individual chapters as self-contained short stories and leaves the ordering of these until the final stages of editing, when he lays the chapters out on the floor and shuffles them around. On the other hand there are writers like Elizabeth George, the American author of the Inspector Lynley crime novels, who before starting a first draft goes through a process of questioning, listing and planning – what she calls 'expanding the idea', writing a 'step outline' and then writing a 'running plot outline' (George 2004: 63). During this preparation she is trying to find out exactly what *kind* of story she wants to write (George 2004: 55).

Activity 9.3   Writing

Make a plan for a story, in note form, connected to one of the following topics (use up to two pages):

- moving house;
- door to door selling;
- the dawn;
- a funeral.

Don't use these topics as your title. Try inventing your own. You are planning for a 500 word story. In the plan list some of the elements you might need:

- character(s);
- setting;
- point of view;
- the dramatic present;
- backstory;
- habitual behaviour;
- some degree of mystery;
- where the narrative would end;
- where the narrative would start.

For example, your story might be about a house move that goes wrong in a seaside town. You might decide to begin when the removal people arrive and start loading the furniture, and finish just after they have left – having forgotten the washing machine! The characters of the story might be the house-owners and the three removal men. The mystery might be to do with the fact that the house-owners' teenage son was supposed to be around to help but didn't arrive and didn't even ring to say where he was.

In your plan, try to plot where and when in the narrative you might give particular packets of information to the reader. Draw a line with stations marked at intervals, at certain points bits of 'freight' will be added to the train of your story.

Discussion

Some writers will be well suited to this sort of planning, but not every writer can plan in this fashion. You will recall that Andrew Cowan charted his progress, but after he had written the narrative, so he could be cognisant of what his narrative had already covered. It is a worthwhile exercise, on this occasion, to see if you can organise your thoughts in advance. There will be some level of planning and preparation involved in the writing of every story, but it might not always be as rational or visible as this. For many the act of writing is a process of revelation, where vital details of both content and form are discovered as they go along. The considerations suggested in this particular planning exercise are the sort of components you will in all likelihood have to consider at some point in the writing of any story. When and how you consider these is a matter of personal practice and often down to the particular demands of each individual story.

Activity 9.4   Writing

Now write the story you have planned in Activity 9.3 (up to 500 words). Keep as closely as you can to what you intended but feel free also to adjust as necessary.

Discussion

A plan can liberate the blank page or screen. It can give you licence to start an idea, and also give you a helping hand. By thinking ahead you will have some idea of what to include in the first draft. By forcing yourself into some form of planning you are actually narrowing down the possibilities for a story and therefore honing its focus. It is important, though, to realise that the plan is part of your creation; it isn't something that should be imposed at all costs on the story. In most instances the plan will have to change as you proceed with the writing, as you discover what does and doesn't work. Sometimes it will have to be completely discarded.

Genre and the reader

In any story you communicate with your reader by building up a rhythm of disclosing or withholding information. By moderating what they know you are inviting your reader to use their imagination, to elaborate on the facts they are given and so help create the story. Genre is a parallel form of imaginative communication with your reader. By giving your reader hints that they might be reading a certain type of story, you are guiding their expectation.

From Aristotle onwards there has been a theory of writing which is all to do with the categorisation of literature into different types and forms. The three over-arching, modern day literary genres are fiction, poetry and drama. Within fiction there are also many sub-genres, such as science fiction, romance novels, and historical novels. The list is ever growing, and also includes types of fiction categorised according to the way it is written, as well as according to its content. So there are epistolary novels, written largely in the form of letters, such as Richardson's *Pamela* (2001 [1740]), or *Rites of Passage* by William Golding (1980), which deploys an epistolary journal. *Bridget Jones's Diary* (1996) by Helen Fielding is a popular descendant of this genre. In this way combinations are formed.

Bridget Jones's Diary, for example, is a 'journal' or 'diary' novel, but is also what has become known as a 'chick lit' novel, because it is written by a woman and is about the trials and tribulations of a modern, young woman.

Stories conforming to a specific genre are often regarded as a lesser type of writing, yet generic expectation within the reader is an important tool to be exploited. Most of the stories we have looked at so far lie outside the more obvious sub-generic headings and might be termed 'literary fiction'. Yet even among them there might be a scattering of generic labels. Raymond Carver, for instance, is often called a 'dirty realist' because of the subject matter and the nature of many of his characters – poor, sometimes alcoholic, and often suffering health and relationship problems. Also, as we have seen, 'The Dream' resembles a fairy story or parable.

Genre is a dynamic aspect of writing and reading, not just a pejorative label placed upon certain types of writing. All readers are looking to spot what sort of narrative they're involved in at any one time. Readers aren't naïve creatures. Invariably they are aware of many genres of story; they are capable of picking up on certain clues which school their expectation. They can understand such codes but don't necessarily need the expectation to be fulfilled. It is this play with generic expectations that often fuels their reading enjoyment.

Activity 9.5   Reading

Look at the three extracts of specific genres which follow. In your note-book detail what sort of writing each excerpt might be. Try to identify the features that drew you to this conclusion.

Extract 1

The pebbled glass door panel is lettered in flaked black paint: '*Philip Marlowe . . . Investigations.*' It is a reasonably shabby door at the end of a reasonably shabby corridor in the sort of building that was new about the year the all-tile bathroom became the basis of civilisation. The door is locked, but next to it is another door with the same legend which is not locked. Come on in – there's nobody in here but me and a big bluebottle fly. But not if you're from Manhattan, Kansas.

195

Extract 2

> The year was 2081, and everybody was finally equal. They
> weren't only equal before God and the law. They were equal
> every which way. Nobody was smarter than anybody else. Nobody
> was better looking than anybody else. Nobody was stronger or
> quicker than anybody else. All this equality was due to the 211th,
> 212th, and 213th Amendments to the Constitution, and the
> unceasing vigilance of agents of the United States Handicapper
> General.

Extract 3

> She didn't look crazy, Max decided. At a glance she seemed a
> rather ordinary, could-be-pretty-if-she-bothered country blonde.
> Only there was nothing ordinary about a slender young woman in
> a conservative navy blue suit sitting on a log at the edge of the
> ocean playing the banjo. Not when the yellow-tinged clouds over-
> head held promise of an April downpour, and the wind whistling
> past her ears was lifting her long hair so that it fell across her face
> like tangled silk.
>
> She looked utterly incongruous. Prim conventionality gone mad.
> Max found her enchanting.

Discussion

It's surprising how it is possible to recognise certain signposts and
linguistic features instantly, even though you may not be entirely familiar
with a particular type of writing. These are some of the labels you might
have come up with, along with the elements you might have picked up
on:

Extract 1 – detective, thriller, crime

This is typified by its laconic, world-weary style, and its direct address to
the reader, made famous by so many movie adaptation voice-overs.
The name on the door rather gives it away. The place is 'shabby' and the
general ambience, as illustrated by the fly, is seedy. One presumes there

is a dingy crime about to land on Marlowe's dingy desk. This is from Raymond Chandler's *Little Sister* (Chandler 1955 [1949]: 5).

Extract 2 – science fiction, futuristic

This gives the futuristic year in which it is set straightaway, but the reader gets no other establishment of time or location. It focuses almost comically on a commonly held, present-day ideal (equality for all), while referring to present-day political language (for example 'Amendments', 'Constitution'). The sentences are short, full of rhythmic repetitions and ostensibly straightforward. This is Kurt Vonnegut's short story 'Harrison Bergeron' (Vonnegut 1979 [1968]: 19). Interestingly it might provoke more generic labels. For instance, it might be classed as 'satire', or even 'dystopian', because it seems to be treating a possible utopian future with cynicism and irony.

Extract 3 – romance, love story

This is taken up completely with the description of a woman, and in particular details the woman's appearance in comparison to what might be deemed 'ordinary' or 'pretty'. The elemental forces of romance, the wind and the ocean, are also introduced here, together crucially with a man's approving gaze. This is Kay Gregory's *Man of the Mountains*, a Mills and Boon romance (Gregory 1993: 5).

Genre and the writer

The important thing for you as a writer is to be able to use some of these generic possibilities when and if you need to. You should be aware of such elements, and not use them accidentally. These are just three examples; there are many more genres that form part of our reading experience.

Activity 9.6   Writing

Now choose another of the starter topics from the list in Activity 9.3 and write the beginning of a story (up to 200 words) around this topic, choosing a particular genre. It doesn't have to be one of those exemplified above though; you might choose epistolary, historical, chick lit, or any number of different possibilities.

As an example, you might choose 'the dawn' in a science fiction genre. You might give a futuristic date, as Vonnegut does. Your characters might have breakfast, some tablets perhaps, and then wait for the purple sun to rise over the depopulated deadlands.

Discussion

It is always a good question to ask: 'What sort of genre is this story?' Even if the answer is as general as 'It's about childhood – it's a childhood story', the question is still worth asking because it can help you gain a finer focus on your material. Sometimes the answer will be, 'This story isn't of any particular type' or 'It's a new genre.' You might think the story is about childhood but realise when you assess it in this way that there are some misleading generic signs, perhaps the hint of romance, or the suggestion of a thriller. You might like to cut these signs or you might like to make use of them, and keep your reader following that particular line of expectation. In this way genre is a potential strength in a piece of writing because it is another subliminal way in which you can commune with your reader. It's important to remember though that there are dangers from conforming too readily to generic expectations. If you reproduce a genre too conscientiously, rather than writing the story you want to write you are liable to produce clichéd action, characters and turns of phrase.

Activity 9.7   Writing

Revisit the story you wrote for Activity 9.4. Rewrite this story, subtly adding an element from a genre that you think might intrigue a reader. Don't conform fully to a genre as you did in the last activity (write up to 600 words).

For example, if you recall the moving house scenario where the son was missing and the washing machine was left behind in the move, the parents might see the shape of a gun in the overalls of one of the removal men. This might be combined with observations that the men are behaving suspiciously. This would give the story a crime or thriller element, even if the gun is later revealed to be just a tape measure.

Writer, reader and story

In writing stories you will constantly be trying out new techniques and exploring certain writing conventions. As you have seen throughout these chapters, it is important that you take your reader with you on these adventures. Have a consideration for the 'freight of exposition' (as Ursula Le Guin called it), and be aware of how much you are revealing and how much you are concealing as you proceed. The best form of exposition is motivated by the characters and action of your story, so it doesn't appear that you are giving out information at all. When honing your words into the shape of a story be aware of the way certain elements might be read in terms of genre, and be alert to the type of expectation you are generating.

Your readers like particular things. They like mystery and they like suspense; they like to be actively involved in the story. They also like to have key features of a world created for them – characters and setting, for instance – and these features need to be filtered through a consistent point of view. Yet these reader preferences are not parts that, once assembled, simply produce an end product. There is always a synthesis involved, something beyond any possible formula; a coming together of form and content, structure and language, which makes any one story unique. As Flannery O'Connor says:

> A story is a way to say something that can't be said any other way, and it takes every word in the story to say what the meaning is.
>
> (Flannery O'Connor, 1984: 96)

References

Allen, Walter (ed.) (1958) *Writers on Writing*, London: Phoenix House.

Baxter, Charles (1989) 'Introduction' in Robert Shapard and James Thomas (eds) *Sudden Fiction International*, New York and London: Norton.

Bowen, Elizabeth (1965) *A Day in the Dark*, Preface, London: Jonathan Cape.

Brontë, Charlotte (1996 [1847]) *Jane Eyre*, Harmondsworth: Penguin.

Chandler, Raymond (1955 [1949]) *The Little Sister*, Harmondsworth: Penguin.

Cowan, Andrew (1994) *Pig*, London: Sceptre.

199

Cowan, Andrew (1996) *Common Ground*, London: Penguin.

Cowan, Andrew (2000) *Crustaceans*, London: Sceptre.

de Bernières, Louis (2004) Interview with Mark Lawson, *Front Row*, BBC Radio 4, 1 July.

Desai, Anita (1978) *Games at Twilight and Other Stories*, London: Penguin.

Dinh, Linh (2004) from 'One-sentence Stories' in *Blood and Soap* New York: Seven Stories Press.

Fielding, Helen (1996) *Bridget Jones's Diary*, London: Picador.

George, Elizabeth (2004) *Write Away: One novelist's approach to fiction and the writing life*, London: Hodder & Stoughton.

Golding, William (1980) *Rites of Passage*, London: Faber & Faber.

Gregory, Kay (1993) *Man of the Mountains*, London: Mills and Boon.

Hind, Angela (producer) (2005) interview, A215 *Creative Writing* CDI, 'Writing Fiction', Milton Keynes: The Open University/Pier Productions.

Joyce, James (1960 [1922]) *Ulysses*, London: Minerva.

Michaels, Leonard (1975 [1970]) *I Would Have Saved Them If I Could*, New York: Farrar, Straus & Giroux.

O'Connor, Flannery (1984) from 'Writing Short Stories' in *Mystery and Manners: Occasional Prose*, Sally and Robert Fitzgerald (eds.), London: Faber & Faber.

O'Connor, Frank (1963 [1962]) *Lonely Voice*, London: Macmillan.

Richardson, Samuel (2001 [1740]) *Pamela*, Oxford: Oxford University Press.

Vonnegut, Kurt (1979 [1968]) 'Harrison Bergeron' in *Welcome to the Monkeyhouse*, St Albans: Triad/Granada.

Winton, Tim (1995 [1994]) *The Riders*, London and Basingstoke: Picador.

Index

Related titles from Routledge

Writing Short Stories
Ailsa Cox

Ideal for those new to the genre or for anyone who wishes to improve their technique, Ailsa Cox's guide will help readers achieve their full potential as a short story writer. The book encourages you to be inventive, to break writing habits and to try something new, by showing the diversity of the short story genre, from cyberpunk to social observation. Each chapter of the book:

- introduces key aspects of the craft of short story writing, including structure, dialogue, characterization, viewpoint, narrative voice and more
- shows how a wide variety of published writers have approached the short story genre, in order to deepen the insights you gain from your own work
- gets you writing, with a series of original, sometimes challenging but always rewarding exercises, which can be tackled alone or adapted for use in a group
- includes activities at the end of each chapter.

Ailsa Cox draws on her experience as a writer to provide essential information on drafting and editing, as well as a rich Resources section, which lists print and online journals that accept the work of new writers. Whether you're writing as part of a course, in a workshop group or at home alone, this book will equip and inspire you to write better short stories, and make you a more skilled, enthusiastic and motivated writer of short stories.

ISBN 13: 978–0–415–30386–6 (hbk)
ISBN 13: 978–0–415–30387–3 (pbk)
ISBN 13: 978–0–203–96262–6 (ebk)

Available at all good bookshops
For ordering and further information please visit
www.routledgeliterature.com

Related titles from Routledge

Doing Creative Writing
Steve May

What is creative writing? How, and why, is it done?

Creative writing is one of the fastest growing areas of study, essential to disciplines such as English, drama, journalism and media. Aimed at prospective students and those beginning creative writing courses, *Doing Creative Writing* provides the ideal introduction to studying creative writing at university.

This immensely readable book will:

- Equip students for study, summarising what to expect a creative writing course to offer, and so encouraging confidence
- orientate the reader in the field by explaining exactly what is 'done' when we 'do creative writing'
- offer inspirational advice to help get started – and practical advice about how to get the most out of the course as it progresses.

Doing Creative Writing draws on the input of students and their views of what they wish they had known before starting creative writing courses, along with the experience of teachers and writers themselves. It also contains a preface by Stephanie Vanderslice demonstrating the global growth of the discipline and the relevance of this book. Steve May's refreshingly clear explanations and advice make this volume essential reading for all those planning to 'do creative writing'.

ISBN 13: 978–0–415–40238–5 (hbk)
ISBN 13: 978–0–415–40239–2 (pbk)
ISBN 13: 978–0–203–93982–6 (ebk)

Available at all good bookshops
For ordering and further information please visit
www.routledgeliterature.com

Related titles from Routledge

The Routledge Creative Writing Coursebook
Paul Mills

This step-by-step, practical guide to the process of creative writing provides readers with a comprehensive course in its art and skill. With genre-based chapters, such as life writing, novels and short stories, poetry, fiction for children and screenwriting, it is an indispensable guide to writing successfully. *The Routledge Creative Writing Coursebook*:

- shows new writers how to get started and suggests useful writing habits
- encourages experimentation and creativity
- stimulates critical awareness through discussion of literary theory and a wide range of illustrative texts
- approaches writing as a skill, as well as an art form
- is packed with individual and group exercises
- offers invaluable tips on the revision and editing processes.

Featuring practical suggestions for developing and improving your writing, *The Routledge Creative Writing Coursebook* is an ideal course text for students and an invaluable guide to self-study.

ISBN 13: 978–0–415–31784–9 (hbk)
ISBN 13: 978–0–415–31785–6 (pbk)
ISBN 13: 978–0–203–49901–6 (ebk)

Available at all good bookshops
For ordering and further information please visit
www.routledgeliterature.com

Printed in Great Britain
by Amazon